Descendants of Charlotte Watson

Compiled by Leonard
Hendershott
September 29, 2020

Compiled by Leonard Hendershott

Foreword

I create these books using Family Book Creator, a plug-in for Family Tree Maker (FTM). I enter my information on Ancestry.com and synchronize this data to FTM. I then utilize FTM to perform maintenance operations on the dataset including *place name resolving* (describing place names by [country], [state/province/parish], [county], [township/city], [postal address] - up to five identifiers ordered by most specific to most general) which permits the listing of my subjects by location. FTM also has a wide variety of other genealogical report formats which can be accessed to enhance publications. I publish separate nodes as I complete a branch of my family tree (now over 30,000 subjects) and publish them using Lulu Publishing.

This book contains the facts, who, where, when, but not the story of the descendants of Charlotte Watson (1853-1933), my 3rd great aunt. If you can add to our history or have an anecdote to tell, then please share it and help make these stories come alive. Even little things, like your cousin the fisherman who didn't eat fish, will make our story more personal. If you can add to our story, please contact me! I hope to have at least a photo of everyone who is here. It is amazing how often there is a close resemblance for relatives separated by generations.

Leonard
Hendershott
September 29, 2020

Contents

Introduction

The following pages list data for all known family members as of September 29, 2020.

Each immediate family is presented in their own section that contains a graphical family tree as well as a description with information about each referenced person and their children. The child section provides information about the children of the preceding couple. When a child has offspring of their own this is presented in a separate family section for that child. In this case a '+' is used to denote that an individual will appear later in the book as a parent with his/her own children and there is a link to the appropriate family reference number. For children with partners but no offspring the partner data is given with the reference family. Roman numerals, followed by a period, are used to indicate the birth order.

In the chapter titled "Families of the Starting Person" the ancestors of Charlotte Watson are presented in a kind of enhanced Pedigree Chart which displays the graphic representation of their direct-line ancestors and the children of the couple. This chapter contains information about the couple whose offspring are listed in the later chapters.

The chapter titled "Families of the Descendants" provides details (as known as of the publication date) for the offspring of Charlotte Watson. There is a chapter for each generation. Relatives are listed in the order of the nearness of their relationship.

Sources for the information provided are given in the footnotes.

This document reports the details of 88 individuals, of whom 51 are male and 37 are female. Of the 52 individuals with recorded birth and death dates, the average lifespan was 56.71 years. Of these, 33 males averaged 57.79 years, and 19 females averaged 54.84 years. The longest living male was William Albert Paterson (1897–1988), who died aged 90. The longest living female was Charlotte Ann Watson (1853–1933), who died aged 79.

Families of the Starting Person

Charlotte Watson

1. **Charlotte Ann[2] Watson** was born on Monday, September 5, 1853, at Southwold (Death age indicated on death certificate as 81 yrs, 10 mths) in Elgin, Ontario, Canada.[1–7] She was the daughter of Richard Thomas Watson and Ann Young.

    Charlotte Ann died in Elgin, Ontario, Canada, on April 17, 1933, at the age of 79.[5–7] She was buried at Evergreen / West Lorne Cemetery,   24928 County Rd 2 (Main St) , West Lorne, Aldborough Township (Concession 8, Lot 17)   Elgin County, ON in West Lorne, Elgin, Ontario, Canada.[6, 7]

    More facts and events for Charlotte Ann Watson:

    Residence: 1861   Elgin, Ontario, Canada[4]
    Cohab: Richard Watson 42, Ann 40, William 17, Clemington 11, Joel 9, Sarah 6, Sharlotte 6, Joshua 4, Joseph 3.

    Residence: 1871   Elgin, Ontario, Canada[2]
    Cohab: Richard Watson 55,   Ann Watson 57,   Joel Watson 19,   Sarah J Watson 18, Sharlott Watson 18,   Josiah Watson 15,   Joseph Watson 13.

    Residence: 1891   Elgin, Ontario, Canada[3]
    Married;   Wife / Cohab: William H Welch 37,   Charlotte Welch 37,   Ida Jane Welch 14, Sarah M Welch 6.

    Marriages with William Henry Welch and an unknown partner are known.

---

1   Ancestry.com and Genealogical Research Library (Brampton, Ontario, Canada), Ontario, Canada, Marriages, 1801-1928 (Provo, UT, USA, Ancestry.com Operations, Inc., 2010), Ancestry.com, Archives of Ontario; Series: MS932; Reel: 36.
[Source citation includes one media item]

2   Ancestry.com and The Church of Jesus Christ of Latter-day Saints, 1871 Census of Canada (Provo, UT, USA, Ancestry.com Operations Inc, 2009), Ancestry.com, Year: 1871; Census Place: Southwold, Elgin West, Ontario; Roll: C-9898; Page: 6; Family No: 24.
[Source citation includes one media item]

3   Ancestry.com, 1891 Census of Canada (Provo, UT, USA, Ancestry.com Operations Inc, 2008), Ancestry.com, Year: 1891; Census Place: Southwold, Elgin West, Ontario; Roll: T-6334; Family No: 35.
[Source citation includes one media item]

4   Ancestry.com and The Church of Jesus Christ of Latter-day Saints, 1861 Census of Canada (Provo, UT, USA, Ancestry.com Operations Inc, 2009), Ancestry.com, Library and Archives Canada; Ottawa, Ontario, Canada; Census Returns For 1861; Roll: C-1019.
[Source citation includes one media item]

5   Ancestry.com, Ontario, Canada, Deaths, 1869-1938 and Deaths Overseas, 1939-1947 (Provo, UT, USA, Ancestry.com Operations Inc, 2010), Ancestry.com, Archives of Ontario; Toronto, Ontario, Canada; Series: MS935; Reel: 463.
[Source citation includes one media item]

6   Ancestry.com, Web: Canada, GenWeb Cemetery Index (Provo, UT, USA, Ancestry.com Operations, Inc., 2013), Ancestry.com.

7   Ancestry.com, Canada, Find A Grave Index, 1600s-Current (Provo, UT, USA, Ancestry.com Operations, Inc., 2012), Ancestry.com.

Figure 1: Alfred Cushman and Charlotte Ann Watson

Figure 2: Evergreen-West Lorne

Family of Charlotte Watson and William Welch

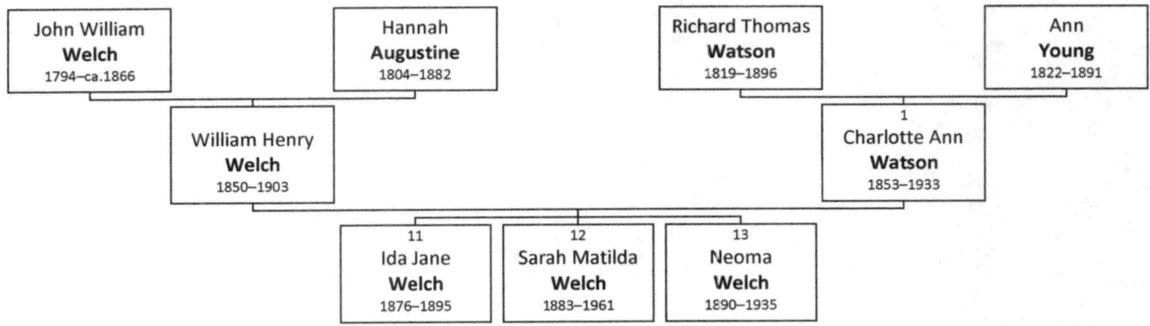

Here are the details about **Charlotte Ann Watson's** first marriage with William Henry Welch. You can read more about Charlotte Ann on page 11.

They had three daughters: Ida (1876–1895), Sarah (1883–1961) and Neoma (1890–1935). William Henry Welch was born at Dunwich, Elgin, Canada West in Canada on Tuesday, October 15, 1850.[3, 8–11] He was the son of John William Welch and Hannah Augustine.

William Henry reached 52 years of age and died in Glencoe, Middlesex, Ontario, Canada, on October 5, 1903.

More facts and events for William Henry Welch:

Residence: 1852   Canada[8]
Cohab: John Welch 58, Hannah 48, Robert 35, Nancy 20, Matha 10, Alexander 16, Samuel 8, Thomas 6.

Residence: 1861   Canada[11]
Methodist / Cohab: William Welch 43, Hanah 35, Sarah C 15, Mary C 14, Harriet Arredatha 12, Eliza C 10, Henry 8, Peter 6, Agnes 4, James E 3, Caroline 1.

Residence: about 1871   Elgin, Ontario, Canada[10]
Cohab: William Welsh 44, Hannah Welsh 46, Harriet Welsh 22, Catherine Welsh 19, William Welsh 18, Peter Welsh 16, Agnes Welsh 15, James Welsh 13, Caroline Welsh 11, Naomiah Welsh 8, Julian Welsh 5, Rachel Welsh 4, Oscar Welsh 2, Olive Welsh 5.

Residence: 1891   Elgin, Ontario, Canada[3]
Married; Head / Cohab: William H Welch 37, Charlotte Welch 37, Ida Jane Welch 14, Sarah M Welch 6.

---

8   Ancestry.com, 1851 Census of Canada East, Canada West, New Brunswick, and Nova Scotia (Provo, UT, USA, Ancestry.com Operations Inc, 2006), Ancestry.com, Year: 1851; Census Place: Caradoc, Middlesex County, Canada West (Ontario); Schedule: A; Roll: C_11737; Page: 55; Line: 36.
[Source citation includes one media item]

9   Ancestry.com and Genealogical Research Library (Brampton, Ontario, Canada), Ontario, Canada, Marriages, 1801-1928 (Provo, UT, USA, Ancestry.com Operations, Inc., 2010), Ancestry.com, Archives of Ontario; Toronto, Ontario, Canada; Registrations of Marriages, 1869-1928; Reel: 36.
[Source citation includes one media item]

10   Ancestry.com and The Church of Jesus Christ of Latter-day Saints, 1871 Census of Canada (Provo, UT, USA, Ancestry.com Operations Inc, 2009), Ancestry.com, Year: 1871; Census Place: Dunwich, Elgin West, Ontario; Roll: C-9897; Page: 50.
[Source citation includes one media item]

11   Ancestry.com and The Church of Jesus Christ of Latter-day Saints, 1861 Census of Canada (Provo, UT, USA, Ancestry.com Operations Inc, 2009), Ancestry.com, Library and Archives Canada; Ottawa, Ontario, Canada; Census Returns For 1861; Roll: C-1018-1019.
[Source citation includes one media item]

Charlotte Watson

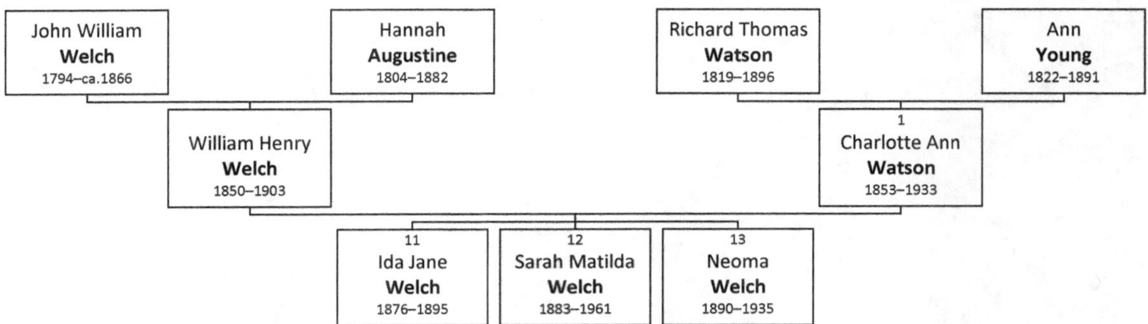

Here are the details about **Charlotte Ann Watson's** second marriage with an unknown partner. You can read more about Charlotte Ann on page 11.

Families of the Descendants

Ida Welch

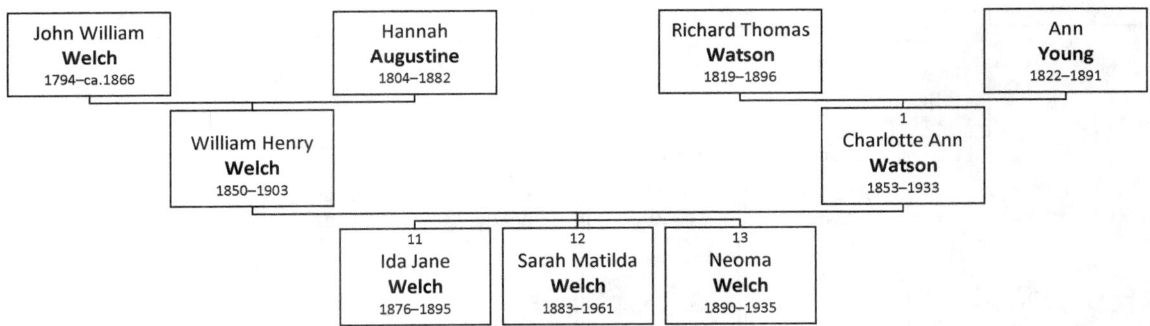

11.   **Ida Jane[3] Welch** was born in 1876 at Dunwich in Elgin, Ontario, Canada.[12, 13] She was the daughter of William Henry Welch and Charlotte Ann Watson (1).

Ida Jane died at Southwold in Elgin, Ontario, Canada, on December 20, 1895, at the age of 19.[13]

More facts and events for Ida Jane Welch:

Residence: 1891   Elgin, Ontario, Canada[12]
             Single;   Dau / Cohab: William H Welch 37,   Charlotte Welch 37,   Ida Jane Welch 14,
             Sarah M Welch 6.

[12]   Ancestry.com, 1891 Census of Canada (Provo, UT, USA, Ancestry.com Operations Inc, 2008), Ancestry.com, Year: 1891; Census Place: Southwold, Elgin West, Ontario; Roll: T-6334; Family No: 35.
[Source citation includes one media item]

[13]   Ancestry.com, Ontario, Canada, Deaths, 1869-1938 and Deaths Overseas, 1939-1947 (Provo, UT, USA, Ancestry.com Operations Inc, 2010), Ancestry.com, Archives of Ontario; Toronto, Ontario, Canada; Series: MS935; Reel: 74.
[Source citation includes one media item]

Family of Sarah Welch and Thomas Beattie

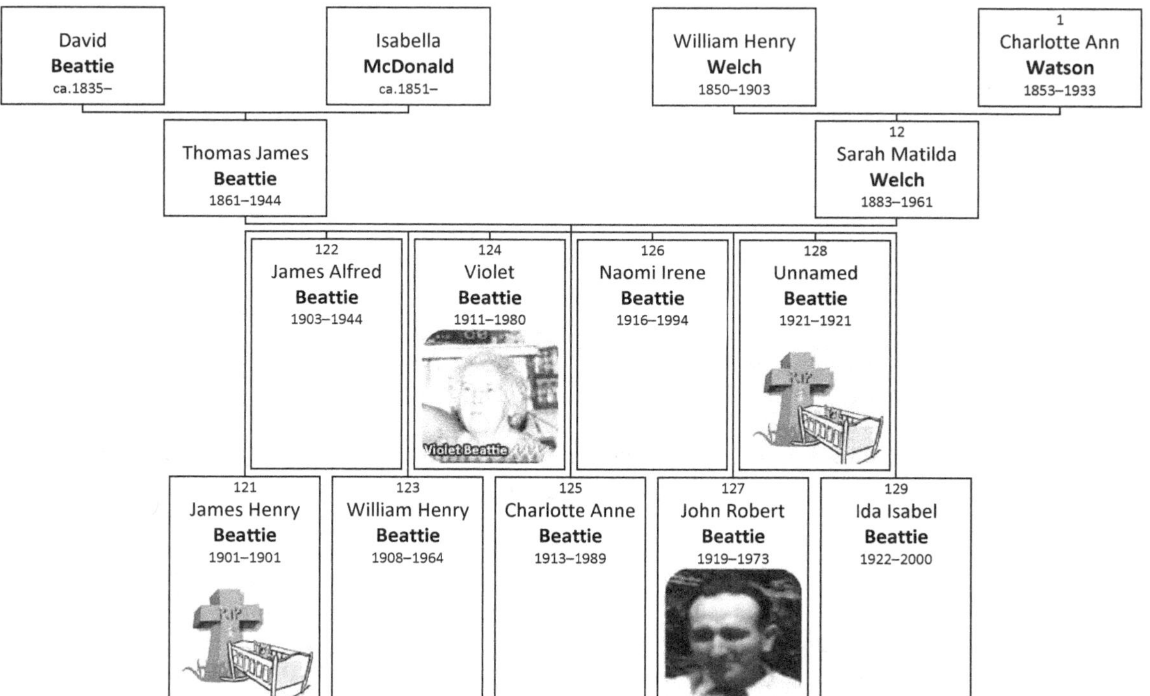

12.   **Sarah Matilda[3] Welch** was born on Monday, October 8, 1883, at Dunwich in Elgin, Ontario, Canada.[14–18] She was the daughter of William Henry Welch and Charlotte Ann Watson (1).

Sarah Matilda died at 414 Edward St in St Thomas, Elgin, Ontario, Canada, in 1961 at the age of 77.[16, 19]

More facts and events for Sarah Matilda Welch:

Residence: 1891   Elgin, Ontario, Canada[14]

Single;   Dau / Cohab: William H Welch 37,   Charlotte Welch 37,   Ida Jane Welch 14,   Sarah M Welch 6.

---

14   Ancestry.com, 1891 Census of Canada (Provo, UT, USA, Ancestry.com Operations Inc, 2008), Ancestry.com, Year: 1891; Census Place: Southwold, Elgin West, Ontario; Roll: T-6334; Family No: 35.
[Source citation includes one media item]

15   Ancestry.com and Genealogical Research Library (Brampton, Ontario, Canada), Ontario, Canada, Marriages, 1801-1928 (Provo, UT, USA, Ancestry.com Operations, Inc., 2010), Ancestry.com, Archives of Ontario; Toronto, Ontario, Canada; Registrations of Marriages, 1869-1928; Series: MS932; Reel: 98.
[Source citation includes one media item]

16   Ancestry.com, Web: Canada, GenWeb Cemetery Index (Provo, UT, USA, Ancestry.com Operations, Inc., 2013), Ancestry.com.

17   Ancestry.com, 1911 Census of Canada (Provo, UT, USA, Ancestry.com Operations Inc, 2006), Ancestry.com, Year: 1911; Census Place: 30 - Orford Township, Highate Village, Kent East, Ontario; Page: 12; Family No: 147.
[Source citation includes one media item]

18   Ancestry.com, 1921 Census of Canada (Provo, UT, USA, Ancestry.com Operations Inc, 2013), Ancestry.com, Reference Number: RG 31; Folder Number: 55; Census Place: St Thomas (City), Elgin West, Ontario; Page Number: 22.
[Source citation includes one media item]

19   Ancestry.com, Beta: Newspapers.com Obituary Index, 1940-1955 (Lehi, UT, USA, Ancestry.com Operations Inc, 2019), Ancestry.com, Times Colonist; Publication Date: 15/ Feb/ 1946; Publication Place: Victoria, British Columbia, Canada; URL: https://www.newspapers.com/image/505993728/?article=c89aa0c3-f9c3-479e-ad85-2dee55c7eeac&focus=0.5024246,0.5848185,0.6144049, 0.74527746&xid=2378.

Residence: 1911   Kent, Ontario, Canada[17]
Married; Wife / Cohab: Thomas Berthe 37, Sarah Berthe 27, James A Berthe 8, William H Berthe 2, Viola Berthe 4/12.

Residence: June 1, 1921 St Thomas, Elgin, Ontario, Canada[18]
Married; Wife / Cohab: Thomas Beattie 62, Sarah Beattie 48, James Beattie 18, William Beattie 14, Viola Beattie 10, Lottie Beattie 8, Neoma Beattie 6, John Beattie 1.

They had nine children: James (1901–1901), James (1903–1944), William (1908–1964), Violet (1911–1980), Charlotte (1913–1989), Naomi (1916–1994), John (1919–1973), Unnamed (1921–1921) and Ida (1922–2000). Thomas James Beattie was born at St Marys in Oxford, Ontario, Canada, on Friday, January 18, 1861.[15–18, 20–21] He was the son of David Beattie and Isabella McDonald.

Thomas James reached 83 years of age and died in St Thomas, Elgin, Ontario, Canada, on October 8, 1944.[16, 21] He was buried in St Thomas, Elgin, Ontario, Canada.[16]

More facts and events for Thomas James Beattie:

Residence: 1891   Elgin, Ontario, Canada[20]
Single; Son; farm labourer / Cohab: Isabell Beattie 40, Thomas J Beattie 25, Lizzie Beattie 23, John Henry Beattie 21, Mary Ella Beattie 15.

Residence: 1902   St Thomas, Elgin, Ontario, Canada
Residence cited in father's obituary. Employed by Griffin Coal and Ice Company until 1934.

Residence: 1911   Kent, Ontario, Canada[17]
Married; Head; Labourer / Cohab: Thomas Berthe 37, Sarah Berthe 27, James A Berthe 8, William H Berthe 2, Viola Berthe 4/12.

Residence: June 1, 1921 St Thomas, Elgin, Ontario, Canada[18]
Married; Head; Labourer / Cohab: Thomas Beattie 62, Sarah Beattie 48, James Beattie 18, William Beattie 14, Viola Beattie 10, Lottie Beattie 8, Neoma Beattie 6, John Beattie 1.

Residence: 1940   Elgin, Ontario, Canada
Residence cited in father's obituary.

---

20 Ancestry.com, 1891 Census of Canada (Provo, UT, USA, Ancestry.com Operations Inc, 2008), Ancestry.com, Year: 1891; Census Place: Southwold, Elgin West, Ontario; Roll: T-6334; Family No: 151.
[Source citation includes one media item]

21 Ancestry.com, Ontario, Canada, Deaths, 1869-1938 and Deaths Overseas, 1939-1947 (Provo, UT, USA, Ancestry.com Operations Inc, 2010), Ancestry.com, Archives of Ontario; Toronto, Ontario, Canada; Collection: Registrations of Deaths, 1944; Reference Number: RG 80-08-0-2350.
[Source citation includes one media item]

Figure 3: St Thomas Cemetery

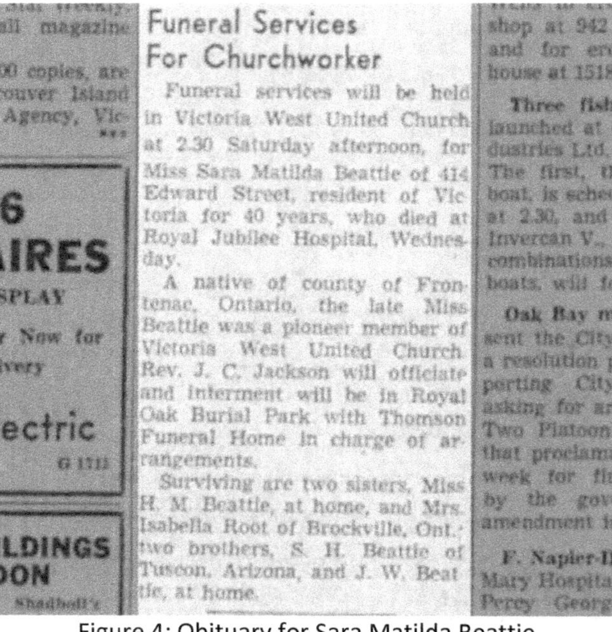

Funeral Services For Churchworker

Funeral services will be held in Victoria West United Church at 2.30 Saturday afternoon, for Miss Sara Matilda Beattie of 414 Edward Street, resident of Victoria for 40 years, who died at Royal Jubilee Hospital, Wednesday.

A native of county of Frontenac, Ontario, the late Miss Beattie was a pioneer member of Victoria West United Church. Rev. J. C. Jackson will officiate and interment will be in Royal Oak Burial Park with Thomson Funeral Home in charge of arrangements.

Surviving are two sisters, Miss H. M. Beattie, at home, and Mrs. Isabella Root of Brockville, Ont., two brothers, S. H. Beattie of Tuscon, Arizona, and J. W. Beattie, at home.

Figure 4: Obituary for Sara Matilda Beattie
(February 15, 1946)

Figure 5: Sarah M Beattie Gravestone
(August 2008)
St Thomas West Avenue Cemetery, St Thomas, Yarmouth Township, Elgin, Ontario, Canada.   Inscription: BEATTIE / SARAH M. BEATTIE / 1882-1961 {Photo courtesy of Darlene Ethel Elenor (nee McCann-Ballantyne) Bateman}

Figure 6: Sarah Matilda (nee Welch)   Beattie Gravestone
(August 2008)
St Thomas, West Avenue Cemetery, St Thomas, Yarmouth Township, Elgin, Ontario, Canada.   Inscription: BEATIE / SARAH M. BEATTIE / 1882-1961 {Photo courtesy of Darlene Ethel Elenor (nee McCann-Ballantyne) Bateman.

James Beattie

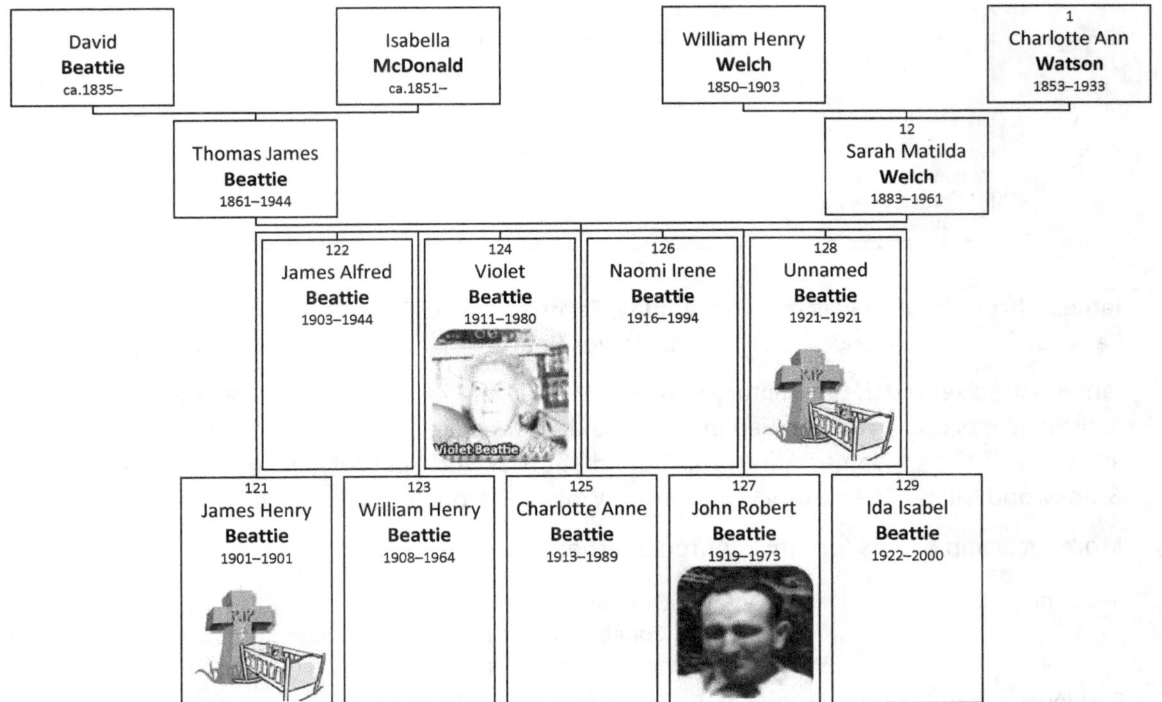

121. **James Henry[4] Beattie** was born on Friday, January 25, 1901, at Caradoc in Middlesex, Ontario, Canada.[22, 23] He was the son of Thomas James Beattie and Sarah Matilda Welch (12).

James Henry died at Caradoc in Middlesex, Ontario, Canada, on January 26, 1901.[22]

James Henry Beattie

---

22   Ancestry.com, Ontario, Canada, Deaths, 1869-1938 and Deaths Overseas, 1939-1947 (Provo, UT, USA, Ancestry.com Operations Inc, 2010), Ancestry.com, Archives of Ontario; Toronto, Ontario, Canada; Series: MS935; Reel: 102.
[Source citation includes one media item]

23   Ancestry.com, Ontario, Canada Births, 1869-1913 (Provo, UT, USA, Ancestry.com Operations Inc, 2010), Ancestry.com, Archives of Ontario; Series: MS929; Reel: 154.
[Source citation includes one media item]

Family of James Beattie and Mary Thomson

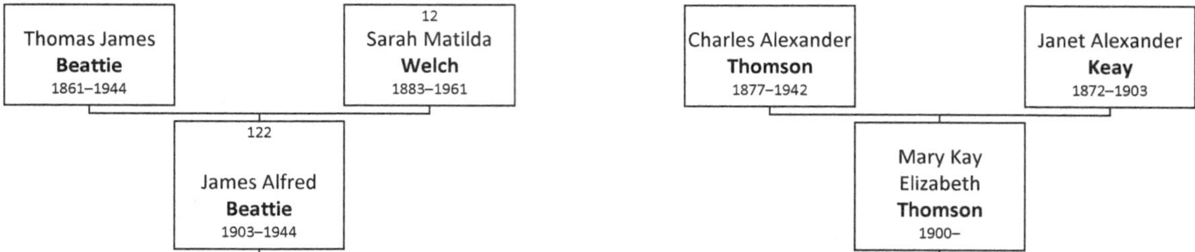

122. **James Alfred[4] Beattie** was born on Sunday, February 15, 1903, in West Lorne, Elgin, Ontario, Canada.[24–29] He was the son of Thomas James Beattie and Sarah Matilda Welch (12).

James Alfred served in the military between 1940 and 1944. Army: Royal Canadian Engineers, 7 Artisan Works Company. He died in Petersfield, Hampshire, England, on October 26, 1944, at the age of 41.[26–28, 30–31] James Alfred was buried at Brookwood in Woking, Surrey, England.[30] Brookwood Military Cemetery, Brookwood Woking Borough Surrey, England Plot: 55. H. 4.

More facts and events for James Alfred Beattie:

Residence: 1911   Kent, Ontario, Canada[24]
Single; Son / Cohab: Thomas Berthe 37, Sarah Berthe 27, James A Berthe 8, William H Berthe 2, Viola Berthe 4/12.

Residence: June 1, 1921   St Thomas, Elgin, Ontario, Canada[25]
Single; Son / Cohab: Thomas Beattie 62, Sarah Beattie 48, James Beattie 18, William Beattie 14, Viola Beattie 10, Lottie Beattie 8, Neoma Beattie 6, John Beattie 1.

Residence: 1937   St Thomas, Elgin, Ontario, Canada[29]

Mary Kay Elizabeth Thomson was born in Dundee, Angus, Scotland, on Tuesday, November 13, 1900.[29] She is the daughter of Charles Alexander Thomson and Janet Alexander Keay.

---

[24] Ancestry.com, 1911 Census of Canada (Provo, UT, USA, Ancestry.com Operations Inc, 2006), Ancestry.com, Year: 1911; Census Place: 30 - Orford Township, Highate Village, Kent East, Ontario; Page: 12; Family No: 147.
[Source citation includes one media item]

[25] Ancestry.com, 1921 Census of Canada (Provo, UT, USA, Ancestry.com Operations Inc, 2013), Ancestry.com, Reference Number: RG 31; Folder Number: 55; Census Place: St Thomas (City), Elgin West, Ontario; Page Number: 22.
[Source citation includes one media item]

[26] Ancestry.com, Ontario, Canada, Deaths, 1869-1938 and Deaths Overseas, 1939-1947 (Provo, UT, USA, Ancestry.com Operations Inc, 2010), Ancestry.com, Archives of Ontario; Toronto, Ontario, Canada; Series: MS944; Reel: 7.
[Source citation includes one media item]

[27] Ancestry.com, Canada, WWII Service Files of War Dead, 1939-1947 (Provo, UT, USA, Ancestry Operations, Inc., 2015), Ancestry.com, Library and Archives Canada; Ottawa, Canada; Service Files of the Second World War - War Dead, 1939-1947; Series: RG 24; Volume: 25406.
[Source citation includes one media item]

[28] Ancestry.com, England & Wales, Death Index, 1916-2007 (Provo, UT, USA, Ancestry.com Operations Inc, 2007), Ancestry.com.
[Source citation includes one media item]

[29] Ancestry.com and Genealogical Research Library (Brampton, Ontario, Canada), Ontario, Canada, Marriages, 1801-1928 (Provo, UT, USA, Ancestry.com Operations, Inc., 2010), Ancestry.com, Archives of Ontario; Toronto, Ontario, Canada; Registration of Marriages Carleton, Elgin.
[Source citation includes one media item]

[30] Ancestry.com, UK and Ireland, Find A Grave Index, 1300s-Current (Provo, UT, USA, Ancestry.com Operations, Inc., 2012), Ancestry.com.

[31] Ancestry.com, Web: Canada, Virtual War Memorial Index, 1900-2014 (Lehi, UT, USA, Ancestry.com Operations, Inc., 2016), Ancestry.com.

More facts and events for Mary Kay Elizabeth Thomson:

Residence: 1937   St Thomas, Elgin, Ontario, Canada[29]

Figure 7: James Alfred Beattie

Figure 8: James Alfred Beattie Gravemarker
Brookwood Military Cemetery, Brookwood, Surrey,
England.   Inscription: A 19568 SAPPER / J.A.BEATTIE /
CORPS OF / ROYAL CANADIAN ENGINEERS / 26TH
OCTOBER 1944   AGE 44 / SOME DAY WE WILL
UNDERSTAND.

Figure 9: Rookwood Military Cemetery

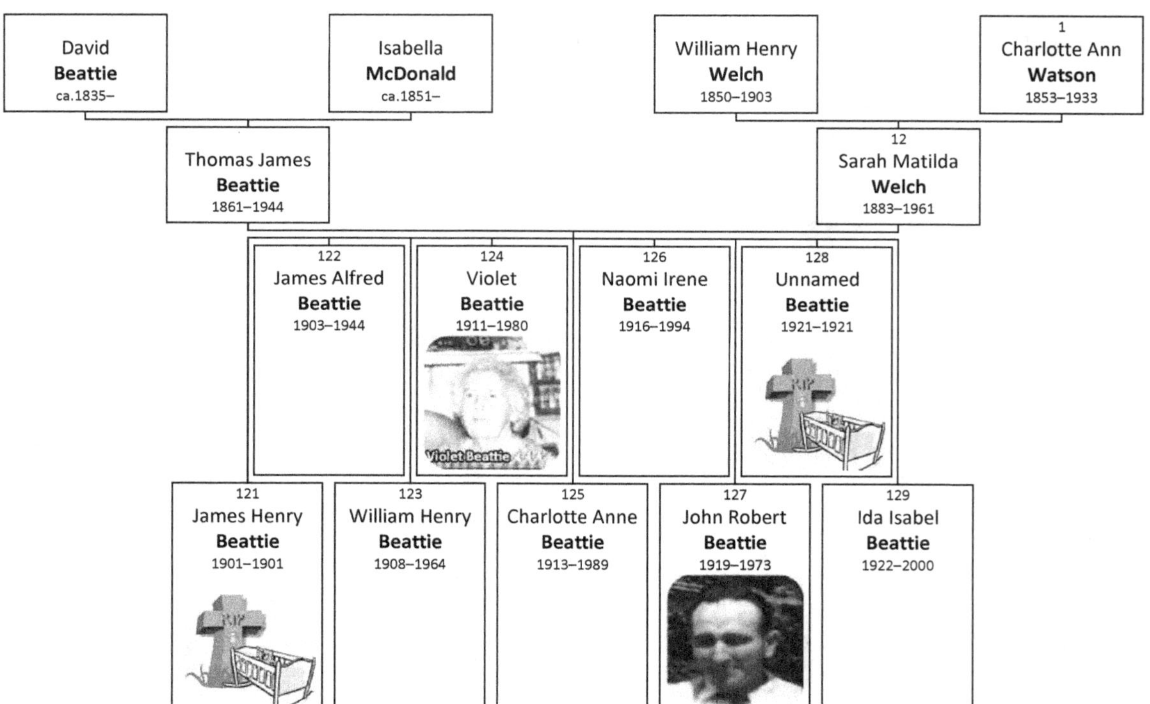

123. **William Henry[4] Beattie** was born on Wednesday, August 5, 1908, at Dutton in Elgin, Ontario, Canada.[32–35] He was the son of Thomas James Beattie and Sarah Matilda Welch (12).

William Henry died in St Thomas, Elgin, Ontario, Canada, in 1964 at the age of 55.[35] He was buried at St Thomas Cemetery, Section: B   67 West Avenue , St Thomas, Southwold & Yarmouth Townships (Concession 8, Lot 2)   Elgin County, ON in St Thomas, Elgin, Ontario, Canada.[35]

More facts and events for William Henry Beattie:

Residence: 1911   Kent, Ontario, Canada[33]
                          Single; Son / Cohab: Thomas Berthe 37,   Sarah Berthe 27,   James A Berthe 8,
                          William H Berthe 2,   Viola Berthe 4/12.
Residence: June 1, 1921   St Thomas, Elgin, Ontario, Canada[32]
                          Single;   Son / Cohab: Thomas Beattie 62,   Sarah Beattie 48,   James Beattie 18,
                          William Beattie 14,   Viola Beattie 10,   Lottie Beattie 8,   Neoma Beattie 6,
                          John Beattie 1.

---

32 Ancestry.com, 1921 Census of Canada (Provo, UT, USA, Ancestry.com Operations Inc, 2013), Ancestry.com, Reference Number: RG 31; Folder Number: 55; Census Place: St Thomas (City), Elgin West, Ontario; Page Number: 22.
[Source citation includes one media item]

33 Ancestry.com, 1911 Census of Canada (Provo, UT, USA, Ancestry.com Operations Inc, 2006), Ancestry.com, Year: 1911; Census Place: 30 - Orford Township, Highate Village, Kent East, Ontario; Page: 12; Family No: 147.
[Source citation includes one media item]

34 Ancestry.com, Ontario, Canada Births, 1869-1913 (Provo, UT, USA, Ancestry.com Operations Inc, 2010), Ancestry.com, Archives of Ontario; Series: MS929; Reel: 4.
[Source citation includes one media item]

35 Ancestry.com, Web: Canada, GenWeb Cemetery Index (Provo, UT, USA, Ancestry.com Operations, Inc., 2013), Ancestry.com.

Figure 10: William Henry Beattie

More figures:
Page 20, Figure 3: St Thomas Cemetery

Family of Violet Beattie and Walter Waller

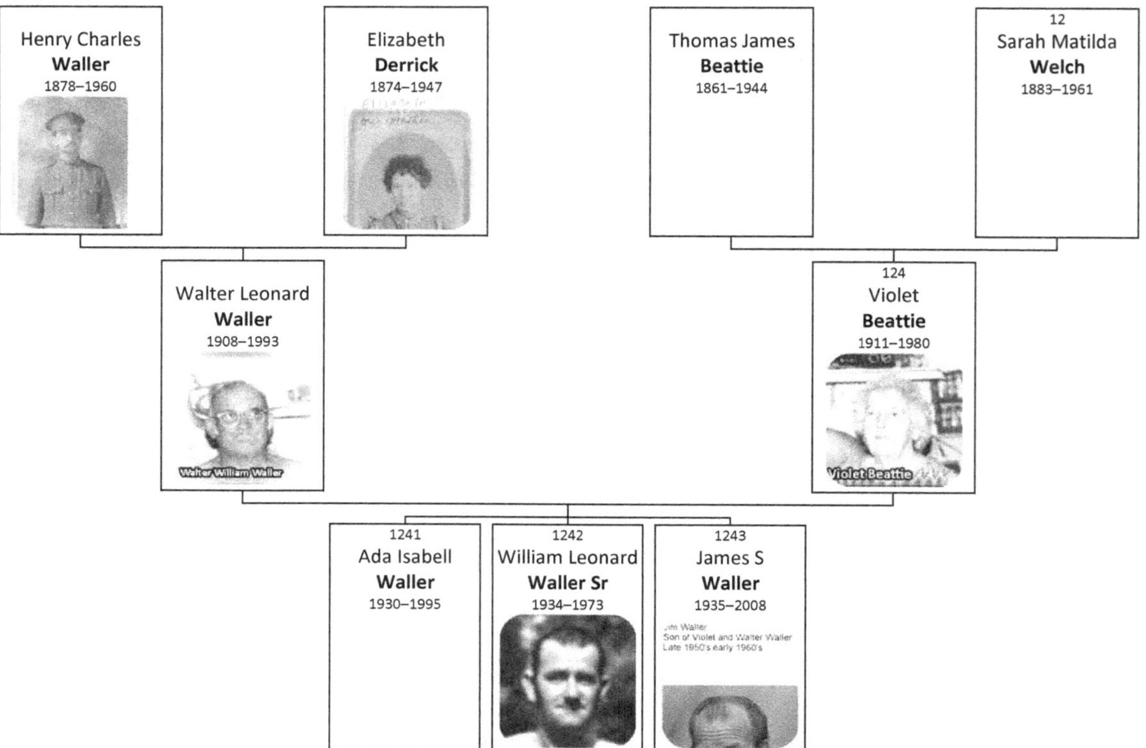

124. **Violet[4] Beattie** was born on Wednesday, February 15, 1911, at Highgate in Kent, Ontario, Canada.[36–40] She was the daughter of Thomas James Beattie and Sarah Matilda Welch (12).

Violet died in St Thomas, Elgin, Ontario, Canada, on December 24, 1980, at the age of 69.[36] She was buried at St Thomas Cemetery, Elgin County, ON in St Thomas, Elgin, Ontario, Canada.[36]

Violet Beattie

More facts and events for Violet Beattie:

Residence: 1911   Kent, Ontario, Canada[40]
Anglican; Single; Dau / Cohab: Thomas Berthe 37, Sarah Berthe 27, James A Berthe 8, William H Berthe 2, Viola Berthe 4/12.

[36]   Ancestry.com, Web: Canada, GenWeb Cemetery Index (Provo, UT, USA, Ancestry.com Operations, Inc., 2013), Ancestry.com.

[37]   Ancestry.com and Genealogical Research Library (Brampton, Ontario, Canada), Ontario, Canada, Marriages, 1801-1928 (Provo, UT, USA, Ancestry.com Operations, Inc., 2010), Ancestry.com, Archives of Ontario; Toronto, Ontario, Canada; Registrations of Marriages, 1869-1928; Series: MS932; Reel: 861.
[Source citation includes one media item]

[38]   Ancestry.com, 1921 Census of Canada (Provo, UT, USA, Ancestry.com Operations Inc, 2013), Ancestry.com, Reference Number: RG 31; Folder Number: 55; Census Place: St Thomas (City), Elgin West, Ontario; Page Number: 22.
[Source citation includes one media item]

[39]   Ancestry.com, Ontario, Canada Births, 1869-1913 (Provo, UT, USA, Ancestry.com Operations Inc, 2010), Ancestry.com, Archives of Ontario; Toronto, Ontario, Canada; Registrations of Births and Stillbirths, 1869-1913; Series: MS929; Reel: 219; Record Group: RG 80-2.
[Source citation includes one media item]

[40]   Ancestry.com, 1911 Census of Canada (Provo, UT, USA, Ancestry.com Operations Inc, 2006), Ancestry.com, Year: 1911; Census Place: 30 - Orford Township, Highate Village, Kent East, Ontario; Page: 12; Family No: 147.
[Source citation includes one media item]

Residence: June 1, 1921   St Thomas, Elgin, Ontario, Canada[38]
Single;Dau / Cohab: Thomas Beattie 62,   Sarah Beattie 48,   James Beattie 18,   William Beattie 14,   Viola Beattie 10,   Lottie Beattie 8,   Neoma Beattie 6,   John Beattie 1.

Residence: 1940   St Thomas, Elgin, Ontario, Canada[41]
Cohab: Walter Waller (Labourer); Mrs Walter Waller

Residence: October 8, 1944   St Thomas, Elgin, Ontario, Canada
Residence cited in father's obituary.

Residence: 1953   St Thomas, Elgin, Ontario, Canada[41]
Cohab: Walter Waller (foundry employee); Mrs Violet Waller

Residence: 1958   St Thomas, Elgin, Ontario, Canada[41]
Cohab: Walter Waller (moulder); Violet Waller

Residence: 1965   St Thomas, Elgin, Ontario, Canada[41]
Cohab: Walter Waller (labourer); Violet

Residence: 1972   St Thomas, Elgin, Ontario, Canada[41]
Cohab: Walter Waller (lead hand); Violet

They had three children: Ada (1930–1995), William (1934–1973) and James (1935–2008). Walter Leonard Waller was born in St Thomas, Elgin, Ontario, Canada, on Tuesday, April 28, 1908.[37, 42–44] He was the son of Henry Charles Waller and Elizabeth Derrick.

Walter Leonard Waller

Walter Leonard reached 84 years of age and died in St Thomas, Elgin, Ontario, Canada, in 1993.

He was buried at St Thomas Cemetery, Elgin County, ON in St Thomas, Elgin, Ontario, Canada.

More facts and events for Walter Leonard Waller:

Residence: 1911   St Thomas, Elgin, Ontario, Canada[43]
Single;   Son / Cohab: Henry Waller 31,   Elizabeth Waller 32,   Ethel Waller 8,   Ada L Waller 7,   Wallon Waller 3,   Charles Waller 1,   Sidney Smith 20,   Nellie Smith 22.

Residence: June 1, 1921   St Thomas, Elgin, Ontario, Canada[42]
Single; Son / Cohab: Henry Waller 42,   Elizabeth Waller 43,   Ada Waller 17,   Walter Waller 13,   George Waller 11,   Rosina Waller 9,   Eva Waller 7,   Violet Waller 6,   Wilfred Waller 2,   Dorothy Waller 1.

Residence: 1940   St Thomas, Elgin, Ontario, Canada[41]
Cohab: Walter Waller (Labourer); Mrs Walter Waller

Residence: 1953   St Thomas, Elgin, Ontario, Canada[41]

[41]   Ancestry.com, Canada, Voters Lists, 1935-1980 (Provo, UT, USA, Ancestry.com Operations, Inc., 2012), Ancestry.com, Library and Archives Canada; Ottawa, Ontario, Canada; Voters Lists, Federal Elections, 1935-1980.
[Source citation includes one media item]

[42]   Ancestry.com, 1921 Census of Canada (Provo, UT, USA, Ancestry.com Operations Inc, 2013), Ancestry.com, Reference Number: RG 31; Folder Number: 55; Census Place: St Thomas (City), Elgin West, Ontario; Page Number: 15.
[Source citation includes one media item]

[43]   Ancestry.com, 1911 Census of Canada (Provo, UT, USA, Ancestry.com Operations Inc, 2006), Ancestry.com, Year: 1911; Census Place: 29 - St Thomas, Elgin West, Ontario; Page: 9; Family No: 105.
[Source citation includes one media item]

[44]   Ancestry.com, Ontario, Canada Births, 1869-1913 (Provo, UT, USA, Ancestry.com Operations Inc, 2010), Ancestry.com, Archives of Ontario; Series: MS929; Reel: 4.
[Source citation includes one media item]

		Cohab: Walter Waller (foundry employee); Mrs Violet Waller
Residence:	1958	St Thomas, Elgin, Ontario, Canada[41]
		Cohab: Walter Waller (moulder); Violet Waller
Residence:	1965	St Thomas, Elgin, Ontario, Canada[41]
		Cohab: Walter Waller (labourer); Violet
Residence:	1972	St Thomas, Elgin, Ontario, Canada[41]
		Cohab: Walter Waller (lead hand); Violet

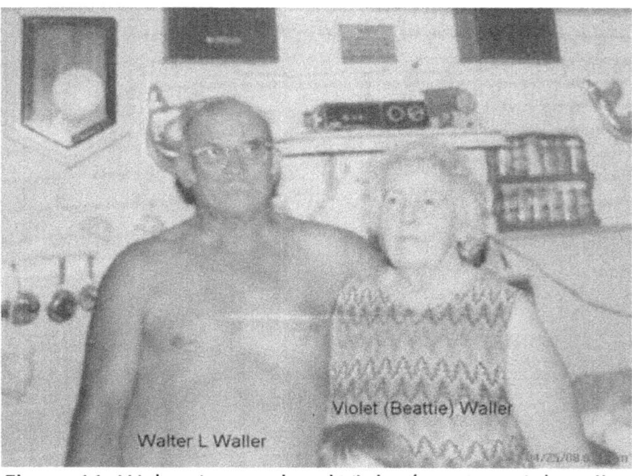

Figure 11: Walter Leonard and Violet (nee Beattie) Waller (about 1971)
Subject: Walter Leonard and Violet (nee Beattie) Waller. Photo snapped approximately 1970-1972 in the kitchen of their residence located at 30 Walnut Street, St Thomas, Ontario, Canada. (Photo courtesy of Rob McCann on 17 Oct 2012).

Figure 12: Waller Family Stone (August 1, 2007)
Punk Waller and Violet Beattie

More figures:
Page 20, Figure 3: St Thomas Cemetery

Ada Waller

1241. **Ada Isabell[5] Waller** was born on Monday, August 4, 1930, in St Thomas, Elgin, Ontario, Canada.[45] She was the daughter of Walter Leonard Waller and Violet Beattie (124).

Ada Isabell died at Wallaceburg in Chatham-Kent, Kent, Ontario, Canada, on February 27, 1995, at the age of 64.[45] Sydenham District Hospital, Per Obit. (Immediate) cause: Heart Failure, Dr.Lorne Thorner, Per Rob McCann. Possible primary cause: Lung disease, had emphysema (heavy smoker most of life, quit abt 8 yrs prior), oxygen user, Per Darlene Bateman + Rob McCann. She was buried in St Thomas, Elgin, Ontario, Canada.[45] St Thomas Cemetery, 67 West Ave., Per Obituary. (Note: Buried with her mother and father, Per Darlene Bateman).

More facts and events for Ada Isabell Waller:

Residence: 1956 - 1965   Toronto, Ontario, Canada
Per Rob McCann. (Note: Lakeview amalgamated into the town of Mississauga in 1968).

Residence: 1969 - 1980   Chatham-Kent, Kent, Ontario, Canada
Per Rob McCann

Residence: 1980 - 1995   Lambton, Ontario, Canada
Per Rob McCann

Marriages with Frederick Percival Stewart, William Angus Buchan Jr (Page 34) and Willfred Hugh Francis McCann Sr (Page 35) are known.

Figure 13: Ada Isabel (Waller) McCann Gravestone
St Thomas Cemetery, West Ave., St Thomas, Elgin,
Ontario, Canada: Ada Isabel (Waller) McCann
1930-1995; Hugh Wilfred Sr 1933-(still living, 2008).

More figures:
Page 20, Figure 3: St Thomas Cemetery

45   Ancestry.com, Web: Canada, GenWeb Cemetery Index (Provo, UT, USA, Ancestry.com Operations, Inc., 2013), Ancestry.com.

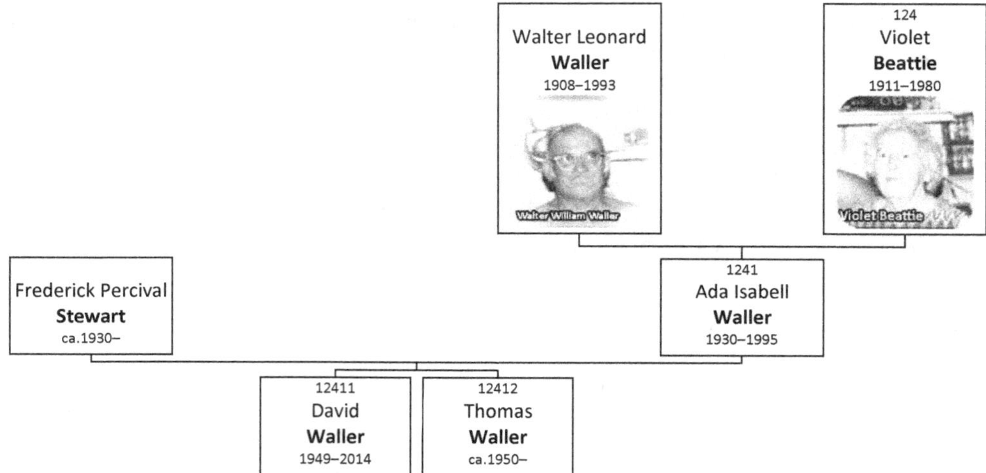

Here are the details about **Ada Isabell Waller's** first marriage with Frederick Percival Stewart. You can read more about Ada Isabell on page 29.

They had two sons: David (1949–2014) and Thomas (ca.1950–). Frederick Percival Stewart was born at (Likely) in Elgin, Ontario, Canada, about 1930.

Family of David Waller and Rose Richmond

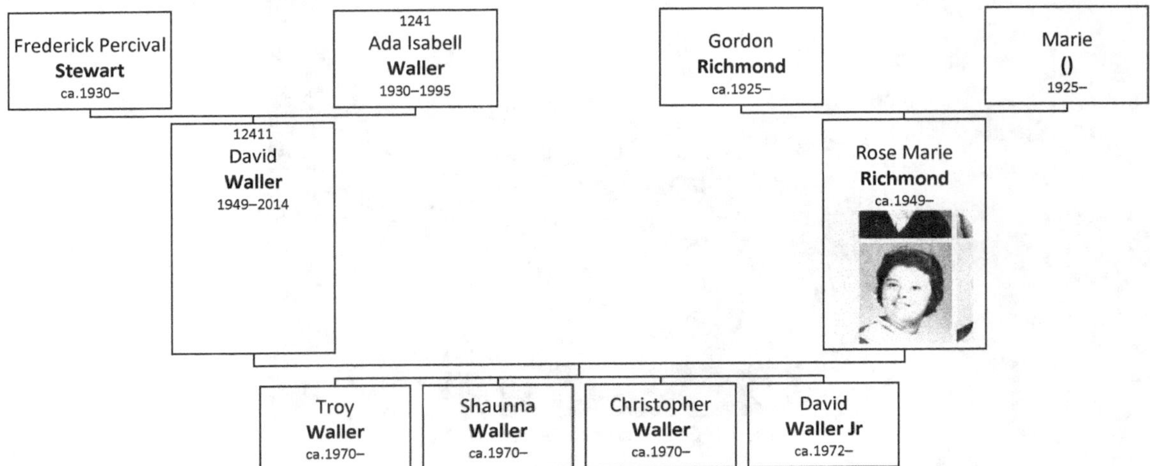

12411. **David[6] Waller** was born in 1949 at (Likely) in Elgin, Ontario, Canada. He was the son of Frederick Percival Stewart and Ada Isabell Waller (1241).

David died at Stratford General Hospital in Milverton, Perth, Ontario, Canada, on August 13, 2014, at the age of 65. He was buried at Greenwood Cemetery, Milverton in Milverton, Perth, Ontario, Canada.

More facts and events for David Waller:

Residence: February 27, 1995   Guelph, Wellington, Ontario, Canada
Residence cited in mother's obituary.

They had four children: Troy (ca.1970–), Shaunna (ca.1970–), Christopher (ca.1970–) and David (ca.1972–). Rose Marie Richmond was born at (Likely) in Elgin, Ontario, Canada, about 1949.[46] She is the daughter of Gordon Richmond and Marie ().

Rose Marie Richmond

More facts and events for Rose Marie Richmond:

Residence: 1967   Chatham-Kent, Kent, Ontario, Canada[46]
Wallaceburg District High School

46   Ancestry.com, Canada, Selected School Yearbooks, 1908-2010 (Provo, UT, USA, Ancestry.com Operations, Inc., 2015), Ancestry.com, "Canada, Selected School Yearbooks, 1908-2010"; School: Wallaceburg District High School; Year: 1967.
[Source citation includes one media item]

Figure 14: Greenwood Cemetery-Milverton

Family of Thomas Waller and Joan ()

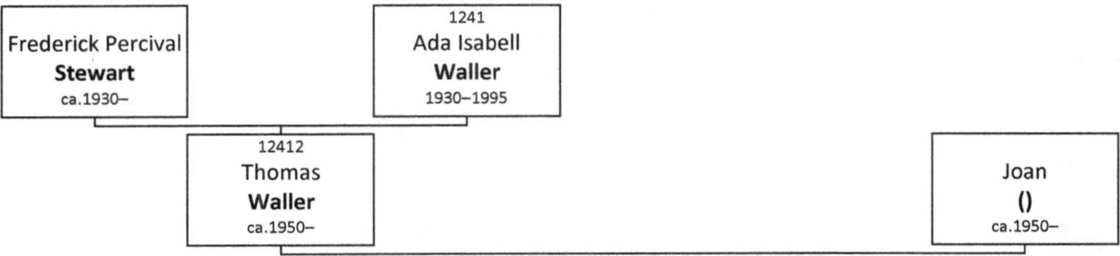

12412. **Thomas**[6] **Waller** was born about 1950 at (Likely) in Elgin, Ontario, Canada. He is the son of Frederick Percival Stewart and Ada Isabell Waller (1241).

More facts and events for Thomas Waller:

Residence: 1974   St Thomas, Elgin, Ontario, Canada[47]
Cohab: Thomas Waller (policeman); Mrs Joan Waller

Residence: August 13, 2014   Elgin, Ontario, Canada
Residence cited in brother David's obituary.

Joan () was born at (Likely) in Elgin, Ontario, Canada, about 1950.

More facts and events for Joan ():

Residence: 1972   St Thomas, Elgin, Ontario, Canada[47]

---

47   Ancestry.com, Canada, Voters Lists, 1935-1980 (Provo, UT, USA, Ancestry.com Operations, Inc., 2012), Ancestry.com, Library and Archives Canada; Ottawa, Ontario, Canada; Voters Lists, Federal Elections, 1935-1980.
[Source citation includes one media item]

Family of Ada Waller and William Buchan

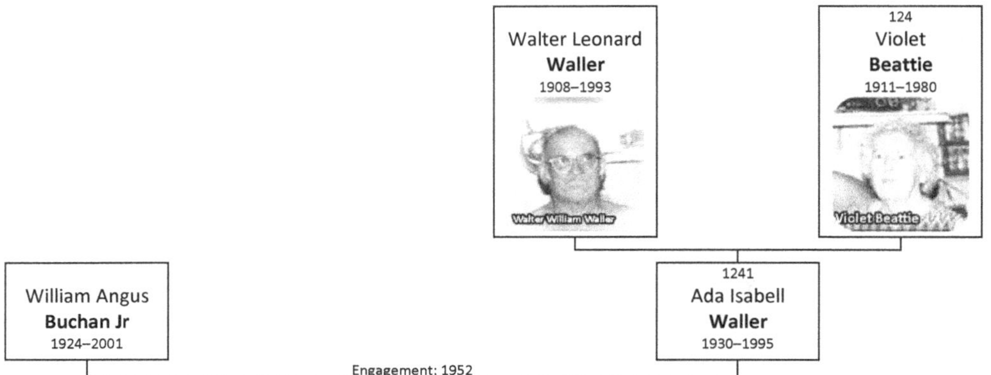

Here are the details about **Ada Isabell Waller's** second marriage with William Angus Buchan Jr. You can read more about Ada Isabell on page 29.

They were engaged in St Thomas, Elgin, Ontario, Canada, in November 1952. Engagement - William Angus Buchan, son of William Buchan to Ada Isabel Waller, daughter of Walter Waller, Per Elgin Cty Branch of OGS, RE: 29 Nov 1952 St Thomas Times Journal (newspaper) Index, p.22. William Angus Buchan Jr was born at Born - William Angus Buchan, son of William Buchan, Nov 9, Per Elgin County Branch of OGS, RE: 11 Nov 1924 St Thomas Times-Journal (newspaper) Index, p.7 in St Thomas, Elgin, Ontario, Canada, on Sunday, November 9, 1924.[45, 48]

He reached 76 years of age and died at St Thomas, Elgin, Ontario, Canada in St Thomas, Elgin, Ontario, Canada, in 2001.[45, 48] William Angus was buried at South Park Cemetery, Elgin County, ON in St Thomas, Elgin, Ontario, Canada.[45]

More facts and events for William Angus Buchan Jr:

Residence: 1957   St Thomas, Elgin, Ontario, Canada[49]
                        Cohab: William Buchan (Ont Hospital)
Residence: 1972   St Thomas, Elgin, Ontario, Canada[49]
                        Cohab: William Buchan (hospital attendant); Mrs Lois Buchan
Residence: 1995 - 2000 St Thomas, Elgin, Ontario, Canada[50]

48   Ancestry.com, Web: Obituary Daily Times Index, 1995-2012 (Provo, UT, USA, Ancestry.com Operations, Inc., 2012), Ancestry.com.

49   Ancestry.com, Canada, Voters Lists, 1935-1980 (Provo, UT, USA, Ancestry.com Operations, Inc., 2012), Ancestry.com, Library and Archives Canada; Ottawa, Ontario, Canada; Voters Lists, Federal Elections, 1935-1980.
      [Source citation includes one media item]

50   Ancestry.com, Canadian Phone and Address Directories, 1995-2002 (Provo, UT, USA, Ancestry.com Operations Inc, 2005), Ancestry.com.

Family of Ada Waller and Willfred McCann

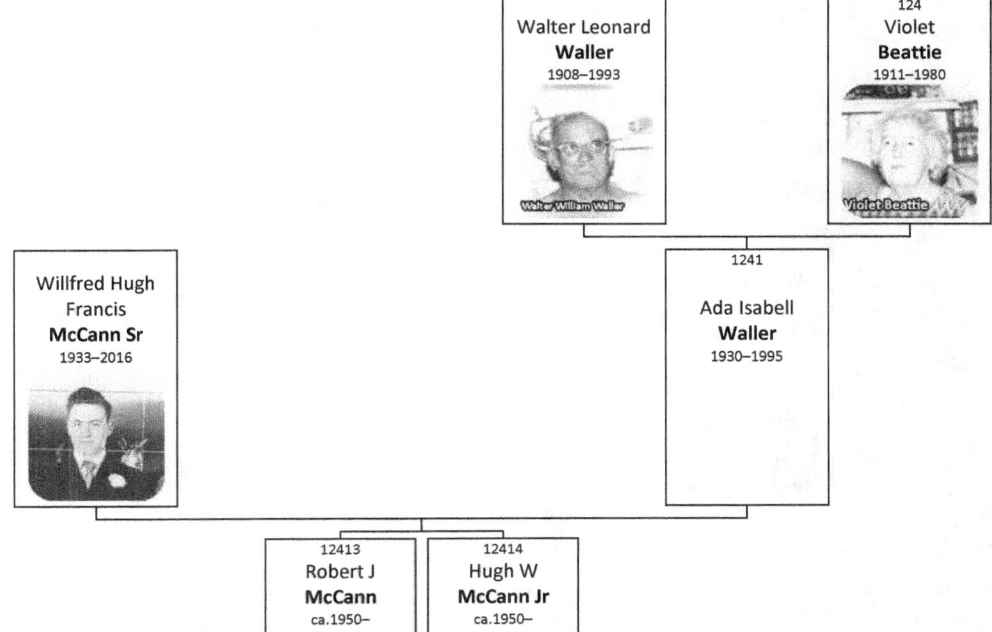

Here are the details about **Ada Isabell Waller's** third marriage with Willfred Hugh Francis McCann Sr. You can read more about Ada Isabell on page 29.

They had two sons: Robert (ca.1950–) and Hugh (ca.1950–). Willfred Hugh Francis McCann Sr was born in Lincoln Park, Wayne, Michigan, USA, on Monday, January 2, 1933.[51, 52]

Willfred Hugh Francis reached 83 years of age and died at Port Lambton in Lambton, Ontario, Canada, on February 10, 2016.[51, 52]

Willfred Hugh Francis
McCann Sr

He was buried at Saint Thomas Cemetery,   St. Thomas, Elgin County, Ontario, Canada in St Thomas, Elgin, Ontario, Canada, on February 13, 2016.[51, 52]

51   Ancestry.com, Canada, Find A Grave Index, 1600s-Current (Provo, UT, USA, Ancestry.com Operations, Inc., 2012), Ancestry.com.

52   Ancestry.com, U.S. Cemetery and Funeral Home Collection (Provo, UT, USA, Ancestry.com Operations Inc, 2011), Ancestry.com, Eric F Nicholls FH; Publication Place: USA; URL: http://www.ericfnichollsfuneralhome.com/memsol.cgi?user_id=1745582.

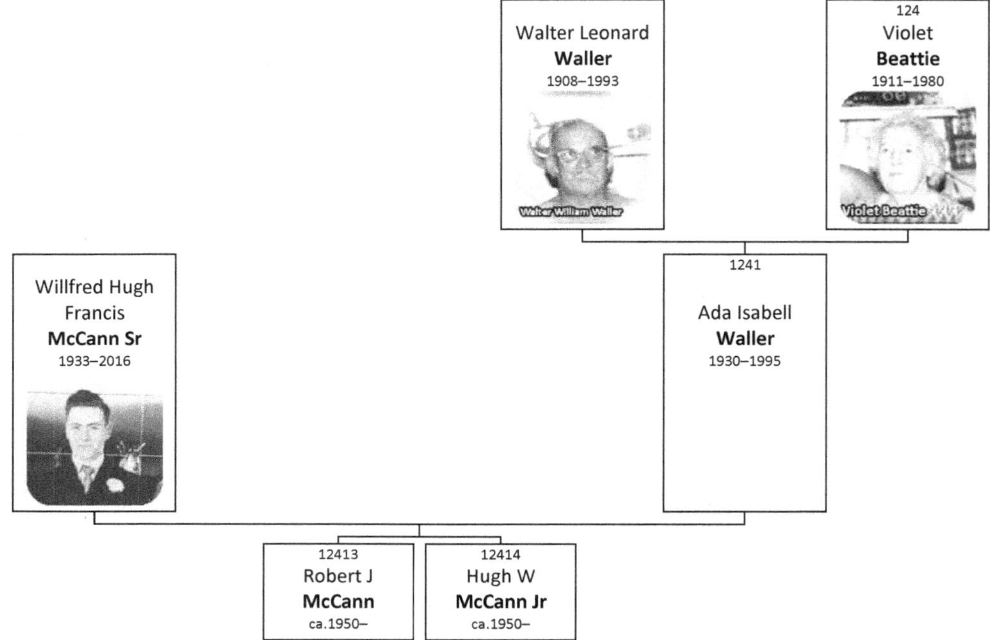

12413. Robert J[6] McCann was born about 1950 at (Likely) in Elgin, Ontario, Canada. He is the son of Willfred Hugh Francis McCann Sr and Ada Isabell Waller (1241).

More facts and events for Robert J McCann:

Residence: February 27, 1995   Sarnia, Lambton, Ontario, Canada
Residence cited in mother's obituary.

Family of Hugh McCann and Mandy ()

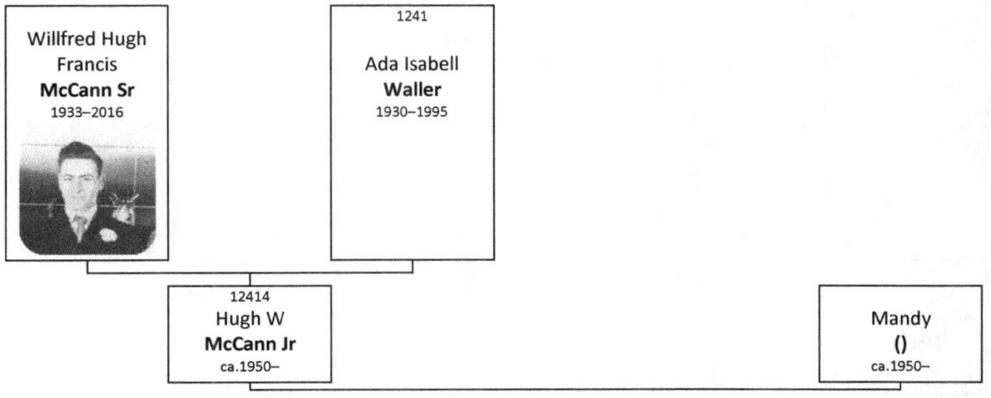

12414. **Hugh W[6] McCann Jr** was born about 1950 at (Likely) in Elgin, Ontario, Canada. He is the son of Willfred Hugh Francis McCann Sr and Ada Isabell Waller (1241).

More facts and events for Hugh W McCann Jr:

Residence: February 27, 1995   St Thomas, Elgin, Ontario, Canada
Residence cited in mother's obituary.

Mandy () was born at (Likely) in Elgin, Ontario, Canada, about 1950.

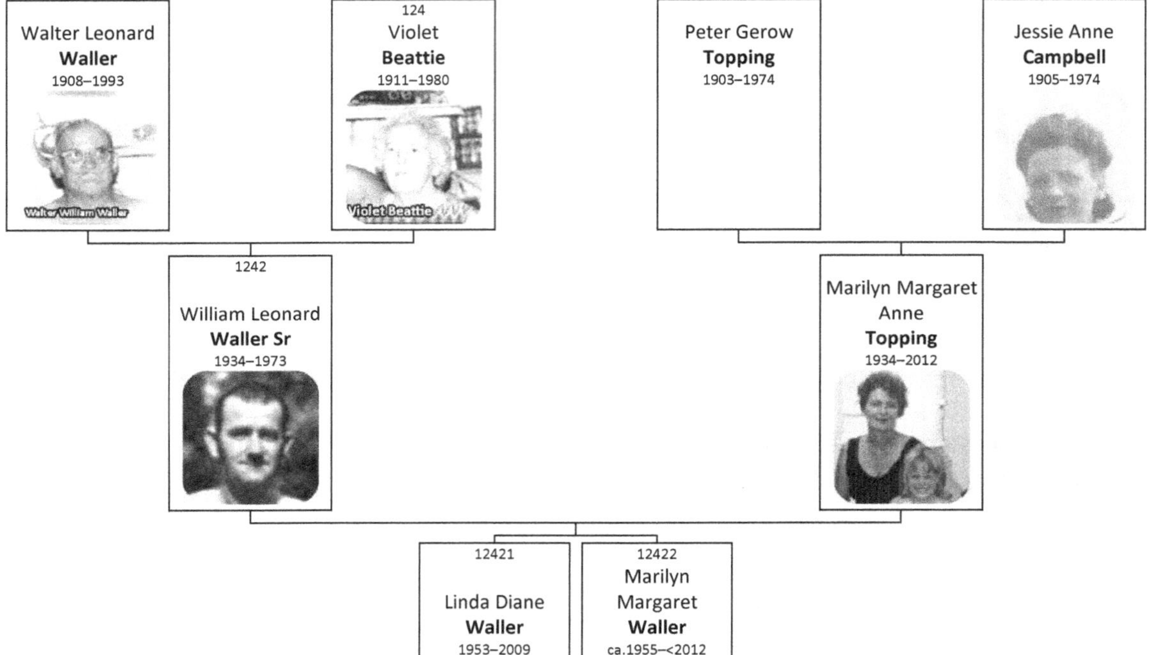

1242. **William Leonard[5] Waller Sr** was born on Tuesday, April 3, 1934, in St Thomas, Elgin, Ontario, Canada.[53] He was the son of Walter Leonard Waller and Violet Beattie (124).

William Leonard died in St Thomas, Elgin, Ontario, Canada, on October 3, 1973, at the age of 39.[53] He was buried in St Thomas, Elgin, Ontario, Canada.[53]

William Leonard
Waller Sr

They had two daughters: Linda (1953–2009) and Marilyn (ca.1955–<2012). Marilyn Margaret Anne Topping was born in St Thomas, Elgin, Ontario, Canada, on Saturday, April 21, 1934. She was the daughter of Peter Gerow Topping and Jessie Anne Campbell.

Marilyn Margaret Anne reached 77 years of age and died in St Thomas, Elgin, Ontario, Canada, on January 15, 2012.

Marilyn Margaret
Anne Topping

Her body was cremated in St Thomas, Elgin, Ontario, Canada.

---

53   Ancestry.com, Web: Canada, GenWeb Cemetery Index (Provo, UT, USA, Ancestry.com Operations, Inc., 2013), Ancestry.com.

Figure 15: Bill Waller
Subject: Bill Waller, son of Walter and Violet Waller.
(Photo courtesy of Rob McCann on 30 Oct 2012).

Figure 16: Walter, Violet & William L. Waller Gravestone Marker
Location: St. Thomas, Elgin, Ontario, Canada

More figures:
Page 20, Figure 3: St Thomas Cemetery

12421. **Linda Diane[6] Waller** was born on Saturday, November 7, 1953. Per Elgin Cty Branch of OGS, Re: St Thomas Times Journal (newspaper) Index, 11 Nov 1953, p.7; Died in her 56th year (a/k/a 1953), Per Obituary. She was the daughter of William Leonard Waller Sr (1242) and Marilyn Margaret Anne Topping.

Linda Diane died in London, Middlesex, Ontario, Canada, on September 2, 2009, at the age of 55. L.H.S.C. (Victoria Campus). Formerly of St Thomas, Per Obituary; Lived in St Thomas most of her life, but moved around after her divorce from Daniel Matiszko, Per Rob McCann. Her body was cremated in St Thomas, Elgin, Ontario, Canada.

More facts and events for Linda Diane Waller:

Residence: 1974   St Thomas, Elgin, Ontario, Canada[54]
Cohab: Dany Matiszko (factory worker); Linda Matiszko

Residence: 1986   Best friend and loving companion of 23 years (a/k/a non-marital relationship) with ALEX COLLINS, JR., Per Obituary.

Residence: 2008   Huron, Ontario, Canada
Residence cited in her obituary. RR 1, Per Obituary. Had lived for awhile in the Windsor area before eventually relocating to Zurich, Per Rob McCann

Relationships with Alexander Collins and Daniel Matiszko Sr (Page 42) are known.

Figure 17: Marilyn Waller Headstone

[54]   Ancestry.com, Canada, Voters Lists, 1935-1980 (Provo, UT, USA, Ancestry.com Operations, Inc., 2012), Ancestry.com, Library and Archives Canada; Ottawa, Ontario, Canada; Voters Lists, Federal Elections, 1935-1980.
[Source citation includes one media item]

Linda Waller and Alexander Collins

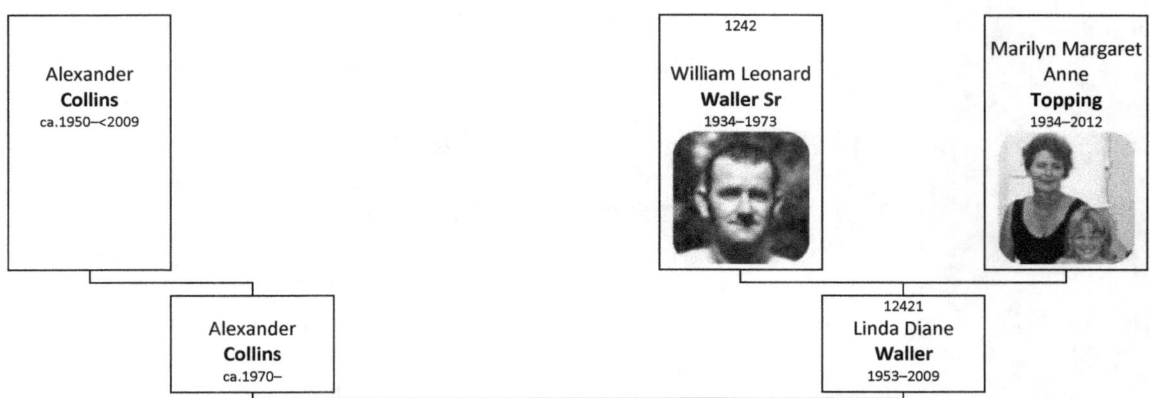

Here are the details about **Linda Diane Waller's** first relationship with Alexander Collins. You can read more about Linda Diane on page 40.

Linda Diane Waller was partnered to **Alexander Collins**. Alexander Collins was born at (Likely) in London, Middlesex, Ontario, Canada, about 1970. He is the son of Alexander Collins.

Family of Linda Waller and Daniel Matiszko

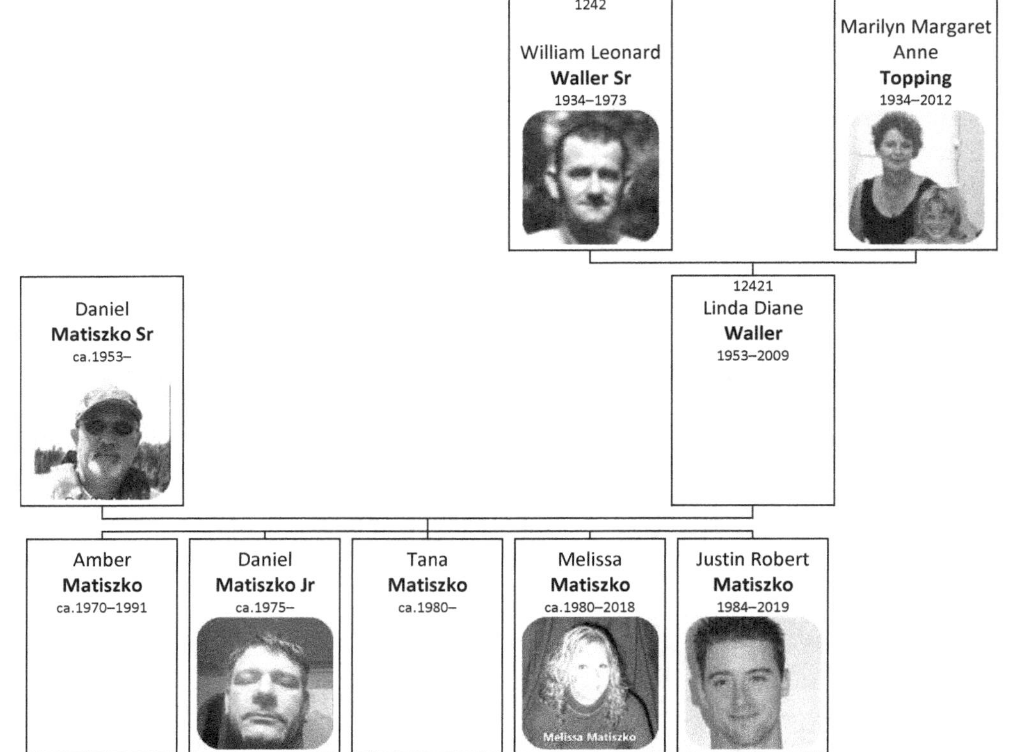

Here are the details about **Linda Diane Waller's** second relationship with Daniel Matiszko Sr. You can read more about Linda Diane on page 40.

They had five children: Amber (ca.1970–1991), Daniel (ca.1975–), Tana (ca.1980–), Melissa (ca.1980–2018) and Justin (1984–2019). Daniel Matiszko Sr was born at Mount Bridges in Middlesex, Ontario, Canada, about 1953.

Daniel Matiszko Sr

More facts and events for Daniel Matiszko Sr:

Residence: 1974   St Thomas, Elgin, Ontario, Canada[55]
            Cohab: Dany Matiszko (factory worker); Linda Matiszko
Residence: 1998 - 2002   St Thomas, Elgin, Ontario, Canada[56]
Residence: 2020   Rodney, Elgin, Ontario, Canada

[55] Ancestry.com, Canada, Voters Lists, 1935-1980 (Provo, UT, USA, Ancestry.com Operations, Inc., 2012), Ancestry.com, Library and Archives Canada; Ottawa, Ontario, Canada; Voters Lists, Federal Elections, 1935-1980.
[Source citation includes one media item]

[56] Ancestry.com, Canadian Phone and Address Directories, 1995-2002 (Provo, UT, USA, Ancestry.com Operations Inc, 2005), Ancestry.com.

Marilyn Waller

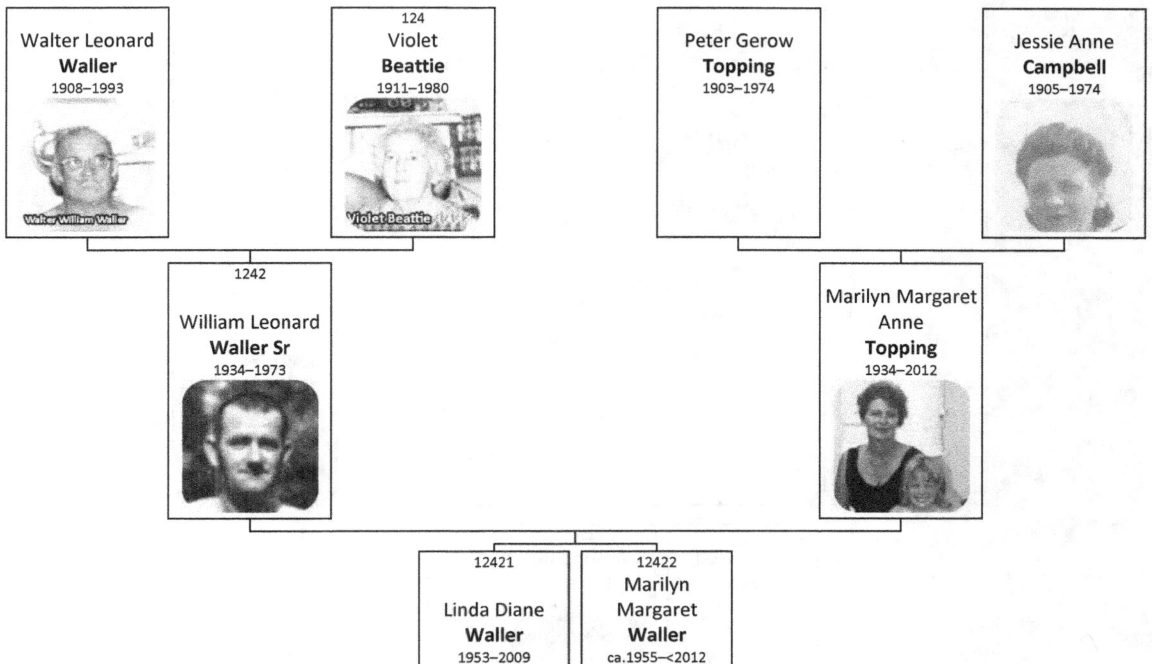

12422.   **Marilyn Margaret[6] Waller** was born about 1955 at (Likely) in Elgin, Ontario, Canada. She was the daughter of William Leonard Waller Sr (1242) and Marilyn Margaret Anne Topping.

Marilyn Margaret died before 2012.

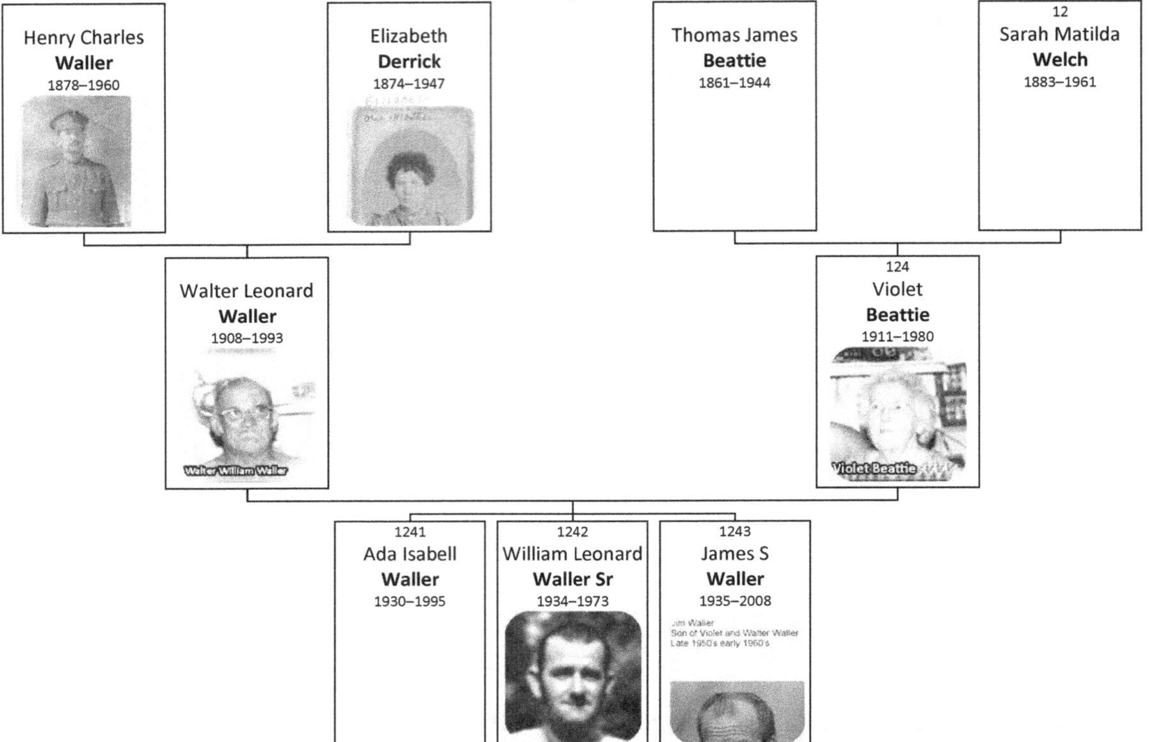

1243. **James S[5] Waller** was born on Wednesday, December 25, 1935, in St Thomas, Elgin, Ontario, Canada.[57] He was the son of Walter Leonard Waller and Violet Beattie (124).

James S died at Terrace (Mills Memorial Hospital) in Kitimat, British Columbia, Canada, on July 20, 2008, at the age of 72.[57] He was buried at St. Thomas Cemetery, West Avenue in St Thomas, Elgin, Ontario, Canada.

James S Waller

Figure 18: Saint Thomas West Avenue Cemetery

---

57   Ancestry.com, Web: Obituary Daily Times Index, 1995-2012 (Provo, UT, USA, Ancestry.com Operations, Inc., 2012), Ancestry.com.

Family of Charlotte Beattie and Alexander McKillop

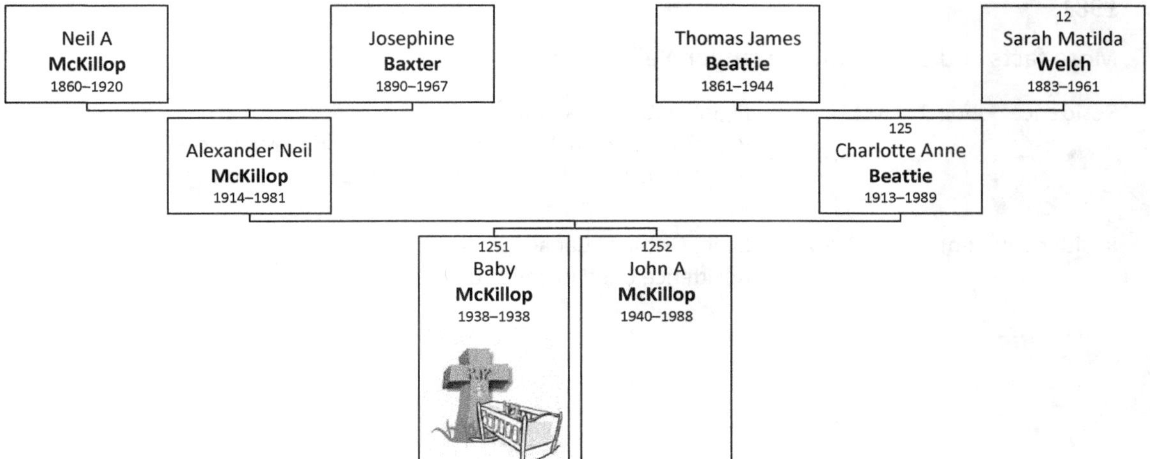

125. **Charlotte Anne**[4] **Beattie** was born on Wednesday, March 26, 1913, at Highgate in Kent, Ontario, Canada.[58–60] She was the daughter of Thomas James Beattie and Sarah Matilda Welch (12).

Charlotte Anne died in 1989 at the age of 75.

More facts and events for Charlotte Anne Beattie:

Residence: June 1, 1921 St Thomas, Elgin, Ontario, Canada[58]
Single;   Dau / Cohab: Thomas Beattie 62,   Sarah Beattie 48,   James Beattie 18,   William Beattie 14,   Viola Beattie 10,   Lottie Beattie 8,   Neoma Beattie 6,   John Beattie 1.

Residence: October 8, 1944 St Thomas, Elgin, Ontario, Canada
Residence cited in father's obituary.

Residence: 1968 Sarnia, Lambton, Ontario, Canada[61]
Cohab: Alex McKillop (C&C); Lottie McKIllop

They had two sons: Baby (1938–1938) and John (1940–1988). Alexander Neil McKillop was born at Iona in Elgin, Ontario, Canada, on Wednesday, July 8, 1914.[60, 62–65] He was the son of Neil A McKillop and Josephine Baxter.

---

58   Ancestry.com, 1921 Census of Canada (Provo, UT, USA, Ancestry.com Operations Inc, 2013), Ancestry.com, Reference Number: RG 31; Folder Number: 55; Census Place: St Thomas (City), Elgin West, Ontario; Page Number: 22.
[Source citation includes one media item]

59   Ancestry.com, Ontario, Canada Births, 1869-1913 (Provo, UT, USA, Ancestry.com Operations Inc, 2010), Ancestry.com, Archives of Ontario; Series: MS929; Reel: 240.
[Source citation includes one media item]

60   Ancestry.com and Genealogical Research Library (Brampton, Ontario, Canada), Ontario, Canada, Marriages, 1801-1928 (Provo, UT, USA, Ancestry.com Operations, Inc., 2010), Ancestry.com, Archives of Ontario; Toronto, Ontario, Canada; Registration of Marriages Elgin, Essex.
[Source citation includes one media item]

61   Ancestry.com, Canada, Voters Lists, 1935-1980 (Provo, UT, USA, Ancestry.com Operations, Inc., 2012), Ancestry.com, Library and Archives Canada; Ottawa, Ontario, Canada; Voters Lists, Federal Elections, 1935-1980.
[Source citation includes one media item]

62   Ancestry.com, 1921 Census of Canada (Provo, UT, USA, Ancestry.com Operations Inc, 2013), Ancestry.com, Reference Number: RG 31; Folder Number: 55; Census Place: 55, Elgin West, Ontario; Page Number: 9.
[Source citation includes one media item]

63   Ancestry.com, Border Crossings: From Canada to U.S., 1895-1956 (Provo, UT, USA, Ancestry.com Operations, Inc., 2010), Ancestry.com, The National Archives at Washington, D.C.; Washington, D.C.; Manifests of Alien Arrivals at Buffalo, Lewiston, Niagara Falls, and Rochester, New

Alexander Neil reached 67 years of age and died at (Likely) in Elgin, Ontario, Canada, in October 1981.[64]

More facts and events for Alexander Neil McKillop:

Residence: June 1, 1921   Elgin, Ontario, Canada[62]
                                  Presbyterian; Single;   Son / HH: Josephine Mc Killop 31,   Sandy Mc Killop 6,   Annie Mc Killop 5,   Arch D Mc Killop 3,   John F Mc Killop 10m, Angus Mc Killop 59.
Residence: September 8, 1938   Elgin, Ontario, Canada
                                  Residence cited in childs obituary

York, 1902-1954; Record Group Title: Records of the Immigration and Naturalization Service, 1787 - 2004; Record.
[Source citation includes one media item]

64   Ancestry.com, U.S., Railroad Retirement Pension Index, 1934-1987 (Lehi, UT, USA, Ancestry.com Operations, Inc., 2017), Ancestry.com, The National Archives at Atlanta; Morrow, Georgia; Records of the Railroad Retirement Board, 1934 - 1987; Record Group Number: 184.

65   Ancestry.com, Detroit Border Crossings and Passenger and Crew Lists, 1905-1957 (Provo, UT, USA, Ancestry.com Operations Inc, 2006), Ancestry.com, The National Archives at Washington, D.C; Washington, D.C.; Series Title: Card Manifests (Alphabetical) of Individuals Entering through the Port of Detroit, Michigan, 1906-1954; NAI: 4527226; Record Group Title: Records of the Immigration and Naturalizatio.
[Source citation includes one media item]

Baby McKillop

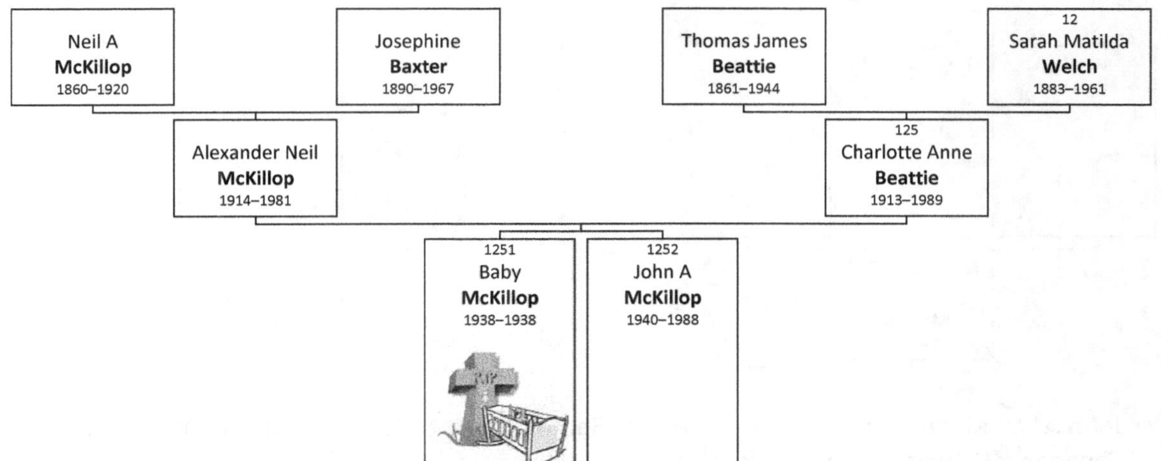

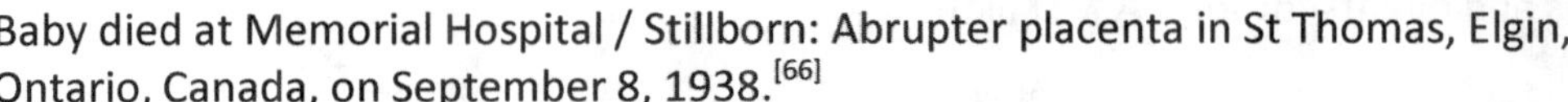

1251. **Baby[5] McKillop** was born on Thursday, September 8, 1938, in St Thomas, Elgin, Ontario, Canada.[66] He was the son of Alexander Neil McKillop and Charlotte Anne Beattie (125).

Baby died at Memorial Hospital / Stillborn: Abrupter placenta in St Thomas, Elgin, Ontario, Canada, on September 8, 1938.[66]

Baby McKillop

---

66   Ancestry.com, Ontario, Canada, Deaths, 1869-1938 and Deaths Overseas, 1939-1947 (Provo, UT, USA, Ancestry.com Operations Inc, 2010), Ancestry.com, Archives of Ontario; Toronto, Ontario, Canada; Collection: MS935; Reel: 606.
[Source citation includes one media item]

Family of John McKillop and Norma Brock

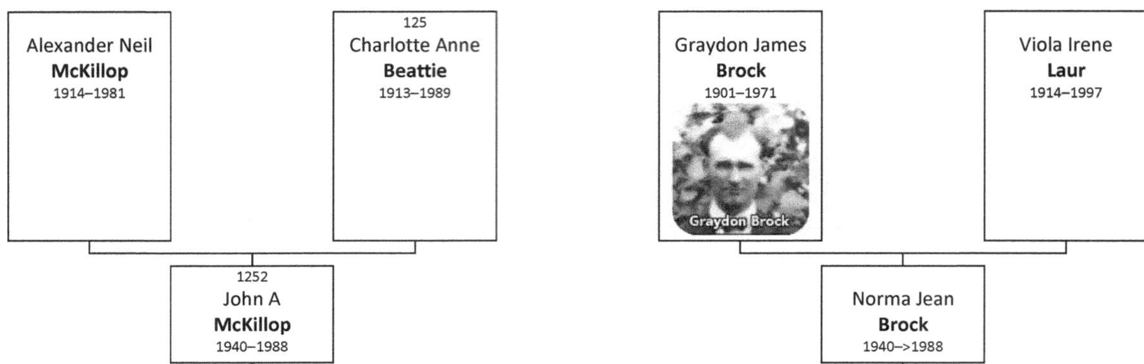

1252. **John A[5] McKillop** was born on Wednesday, September 4, 1940, in Sarnia, Lambton, Ontario, Canada.[67] He was the son of Alexander Neil McKillop and Charlotte Anne Beattie (125).

John A died in Sarnia, Lambton, Ontario, Canada, on November 17, 1988, at the age of 48.[67] He was buried at Wallaceburg (Riverview Cemetery, Wallaceburg, Chatham-Kent Municipality, Ontario, Canad) in Chatham-Kent, Kent, Ontario, Canada.[67]

More facts and events for John A McKillop:

Residence: 1968   Lambton, Ontario, Canada[68]
Cohab: John McKIllop (Labourer); Norma

Norma Jean Brock was born at (Likely) in Lambton, Ontario, Canada, in 1940.[67] She was the daughter of Graydon James Brock and Viola Irene Laur.

Norma Jean died after 1988. Alive at time of husband's death. She was buried at Wallaceburg in Chatham-Kent, Kent, Ontario, Canada.[67]

More facts and events for Norma Jean Brock:

Residence: 1965   Lambton, Ontario, Canada[68]
Residence: 1972   Lambton, Ontario, Canada[68]

---

67   Ancestry.com, Canada, Find A Grave Index, 1600s-Current (Provo, UT, USA, Ancestry.com Operations, Inc., 2012), Ancestry.com.

68   Ancestry.com, Canada, Voters Lists, 1935-1980 (Provo, UT, USA, Ancestry.com Operations, Inc., 2012), Ancestry.com, Library and Archives Canada; Ottawa, Ontario, Canada; Voters Lists, Federal Elections, 1935-1980.
[Source citation includes one media item]

Figure 19: John A McKillop

Figure 20: Riverview Cemetery

Family of Naomi Beattie and Donald Howe Latta

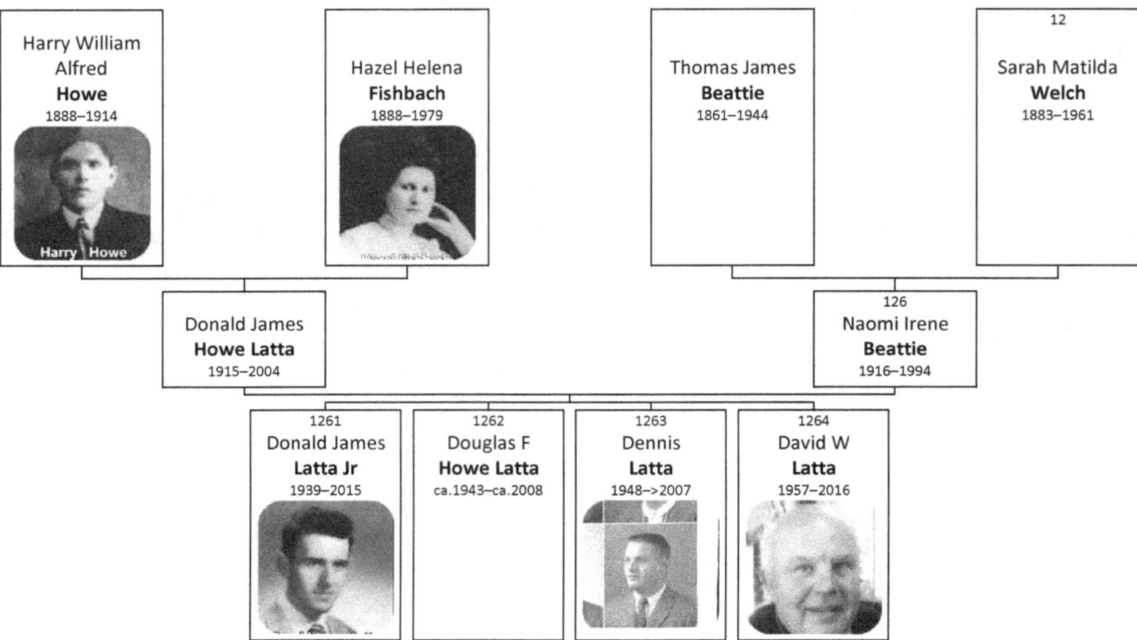

126.   **Naomi Irene[4] Beattie** was born on Thursday, August 17, 1916, in West Lorne, Elgin, Ontario, Canada.[69–74] She was the daughter of Thomas James Beattie and Sarah Matilda Welch (12).

Naomi Irene died in Lockport, Niagara, New York, USA, on December 18, 1994, at the age of 78.[70, 71]

More facts and events for Naomi Irene Beattie:

Residence:	June 1, 1921	St Thomas, Elgin, Ontario, Canada[69]
		Single; Dau / Cohab: Thomas Beattie 62, Sarah Beattie 48, James Beattie 18, William Beattie 14, Viola Beattie 10, Lottie Beattie 8, Neoma Beattie 6, John Beattie 1.
Residence:	1935	St Thomas, Elgin, Ontario, Canada[72]
Residence:	April 1, 1940	Lockport, Niagara, New York, USA[72]
		Married; Wife / Cohab: Donald Y Latta 24, Neomie Latta 23, Donaed Latta 1, Harry W Latta 49, Hazel H Latta 56, Margaret Latta 21, Lorma Latta

69   Ancestry.com, 1921 Census of Canada (Provo, UT, USA, Ancestry.com Operations Inc, 2013), Ancestry.com, Reference Number: RG 31; Folder Number: 55; Census Place: St Thomas (City), Elgin West, Ontario; Page Number: 22.
[Source citation includes one media item]

70   Ancestry.com, U.S., Social Security Applications and Claims Index, 1936-2007 (Provo, UT, USA, Ancestry.com Operations, Inc., 2015), Ancestry.com.

71   Ancestry.com, U.S., Social Security Death Index, 1935-Current (Provo, UT, USA, Ancestry.com Operations Inc, 2011), Ancestry.com, Number: 122-48-5826; Issue State: New York; Issue Date: 1971.

72   Ancestry.com, 1940 United States Federal Census (Provo, UT, USA, Ancestry.com Operations, Inc., 2012), Ancestry.com, Year: 1940; Census Place: Lockport, Niagara, New York; Roll: T627_2695; Page: 61A; Enumeration District: 32-31.
[Source citation includes one media item]

73   Ancestry.com and Genealogical Research Library (Brampton, Ontario, Canada), Ontario, Canada, Marriages, 1801-1928 (Provo, UT, USA, Ancestry.com Operations, Inc., 2010), Ancestry.com, Archives of Ontario; Toronto, Ontario, Canada; Registration of Marriages Elgin, Essex.
[Source citation includes one media item]

74   Ancestry.com, U.S. Public Records Index, Volume 2 (Provo, UT, USA, Ancestry.com Operations, Inc., 2010), Ancestry.com.

19.

Residence:	October 8, 1944	Lockport, Niagara, New York, USA
		Residence cited in father's obituary.
Residence:	1949	Lockport, Niagara, New York, USA[75]
Residence:		Lockport, Niagara, New York, USA[74]

They had four sons: Donald (1939–2015), Douglas (ca.1943–ca.2008), Dennis (1948–>2007) and David (1957–2016). Donald James Howe Latta was born in Aylmer, Elgin, Ontario, Canada, on Monday, April 26, 1915.[70, 72, 73, 76–79] He was the son of Harry William Alfred Howe and Hazel Helena Fishbach.

Donald James reached 88 years of age and died in Lockport, Niagara, New York, USA, on January 14, 2004.[70, 77, 79]

More facts and events for Donald James Howe Latta:

Residence:	1935	Medina, Orleans, New York, USA[72]
Residence:	April 1, 1940	Lockport, Niagara, New York, USA[72]
		Married; Head; roofer / Cohab: Donald Y Latta 24, Neomie Latta 23, Donaed Latta 1, Harry W Latta 49, Hazel H Latta 56, Margaret Latta 21, Lorma Latta 19.
Residence:	1949	Lockport, Niagara, New York, USA[75]
Residence:	1993	Lockport, Niagara, New York, USA[78]
Residence:	1996 - 2002	Lockport, Niagara, New York, USA[80]

Figure 21: Donald J Latta

75   Ancestry.com, U.S. City Directories, 1821-1989 (Provo, UT, USA, Ancestry.com Operations, Inc., 2011), Ancestry.com. [Source citation includes one media item]

76   Ancestry.com, U.S. WWII Draft Cards Young Men, 1940-1947 (Provo, UT, USA, Ancestry.com Operations, Inc., 2011), Ancestry.com. [Source citation includes one media item]

77   Ancestry.com, U.S., Social Security Death Index, 1935-Current (Provo, UT, USA, Ancestry.com Operations Inc, 2011), Ancestry.com, Social Security Administration; Washington D.C., USA; Social Security Death Index, Master File.

78   Ancestry.com, U.S. Public Records Index, Volume 1 (Provo, UT, USA, Ancestry.com Operations, Inc., 2010), Ancestry.com.

79   Ancestry.com, Beta: Newspapers.com Obituary Index, 1940-1955 (Lehi, UT, USA, Ancestry.com Operations Inc, 2019), Ancestry.com, The Daily Oklahoman; Publication Date: 14/ Apr/ 2004; Publication Place: Oklahoma City, Oklahoma, United States of America; URL: https://www.newspapers.com/image/452668685/?article=f1937595-0892-4e0f-8f1b-0304f5330281&focus=0.32380703,0.4914317,0.4941002 4.

80   Ancestry.com, U.S. Phone and Address Directories, 1993-2002 (Provo, UT, USA, Ancestry.com Operations Inc, 2005), Ancestry.com, City: Lockport; State: New York; Year(s): 1996-2002.

Family of Donald Latta and Carol Wolters

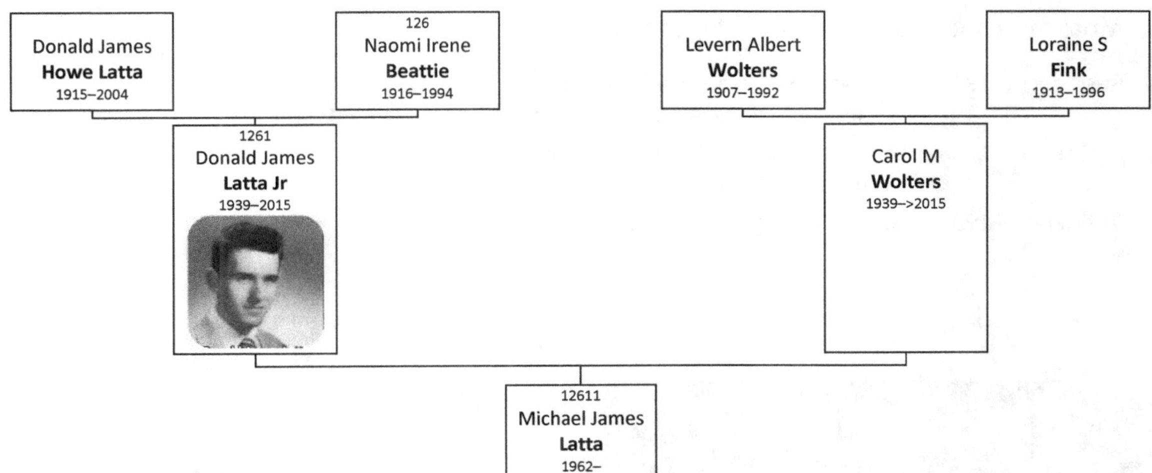

1261.   **Donald James[5] Latta Jr** was born on Friday, January 20, 1939, in St Thomas, Elgin, Ontario, Canada.[81–85] He was the son of Donald James Howe Latta and Naomi Irene Beattie (126).

Donald James Latta Jr

Donald James died in Lockport, Niagara, New York, USA, on April 25, 2015, at the age of 76.[83, 85] He was buried at Cold Springs Cemetery,   Lockport, Niagara County, New York, USA in Lockport, Niagara, New York, USA.[85]

More facts and events for Donald James Latta Jr:

Residence: April 1, 1940   Lockport, Niagara, New York, USA[81]
                              Single; Son / Cohab: Donald Y Latta 24,   Neomie Latta 23,   Donaed Latta 1,
                              Harry W Latta 49,   Hazel H Latta 56,   Margaret Latta 21,   Lorma Latta 19.
Residence: 1958   Lockport, Niagara, New York, USA[86]
Residence: 1993   Lockport, Niagara, New York, USA[82]
Residence: 1996 - 2002   Lockport, Niagara, New York, USA[87]

They had one son: Michael (1962–). Carol M Wolters was born in Lockport, Niagara, New York, USA, on Wednesday, November 8, 1939.[82, 88, 89] She was the daughter of Levern Albert Wolters and Loraine S Fink.

[81]   Ancestry.com, 1940 United States Federal Census (Provo, UT, USA, Ancestry.com Operations, Inc., 2012), Ancestry.com, Year: 1940; Census Place: Lockport, Niagara, New York; Roll: T627_2695; Page: 61A; Enumeration District: 32-31.
       [Source citation includes one media item]

[82]   Ancestry.com, U.S. Public Records Index, Volume 1 (Provo, UT, USA, Ancestry.com Operations, Inc., 2010), Ancestry.com.

[83]   Ancestry.com, U.S. Cemetery and Funeral Home Collection (Provo, UT, USA, Ancestry.com Operations Inc, 2011), Ancestry.com, Lange Funeral Home, Inc; Publication Place: Lockport, NY, US; URL: https://langefuneralhomeinc.com/tribute/details/373/Donald-Latta/obituary.html.

[84]   Ancestry.com, Border Crossings: From Canada to U.S., 1895-1956 (Provo, UT, USA, Ancestry.com Operations, Inc., 2010), Ancestry.com, The National Archives at Washington, D.C.; Washington, D.C.; Manifests of Alien Arrivals at Buffalo, Lewiston, Niagara Falls, and Rochester, New York, 1902-1954; Record Group Title: Records of the Immigration and Naturalization Service, 1787 - 2004; Record.
       [Source citation includes one media item]

[85]   Ancestry.com, U.S., Find A Grave Index, 1700s-Current (Provo, UT, USA, Ancestry.com Operations, Inc., 2012), Ancestry.com.

[86]   Ancestry.com, U.S. City Directories, 1821-1989 (Provo, UT, USA, Ancestry.com Operations, Inc., 2011), Ancestry.com.
       [Source citation includes one media item]

[87]   Ancestry.com, U.S. Phone and Address Directories, 1993-2002 (Provo, UT, USA, Ancestry.com Operations Inc, 2005), Ancestry.com, City: Lockport; State: New York; Year(s): 1996-2002.

Carol M died after 2015. Cited as living on headstone.

More facts and events for Carol M Wolters:

Residence: 1940   Lockport, Niagara, New York, USA[88]
                    Single;   Dau / Cohab: Levern Walters 32,   Loraine Walters 26,   Carol Walters 5/12.
Residence: 1958   Lockport, Niagara, New York, USA[86]
                    Occupation: Clerk
Residence: 1993   Lockport, Niagara, New York, USA[82]

Figure 22: Cold Springs Cemetery

Figure 23: Donald J. Latta

More figures:
Page 51, Figure 21: Donald J Latta

88   Ancestry.com, 1940 United States Federal Census (Provo, UT, USA, Ancestry.com Operations, Inc., 2012), Ancestry.com, Year: 1940; Census Place: Lockport, Niagara, New York; Roll: m-t0627-02695; Page: 6A; Enumeration District: 32-27.
      [Source citation includes one media item]

89   Ancestry.com, New York State, Birth Index, 1881-1942 (Lehi, UT, USA, Ancestry.com Operations, Inc., 2018), Ancestry.com, New York State Department of Health; Albany, NY, USA; New York State Birth Index.
      [Source citation includes one media item]

Family of Michael Latta and Bonnie Fitzgerald

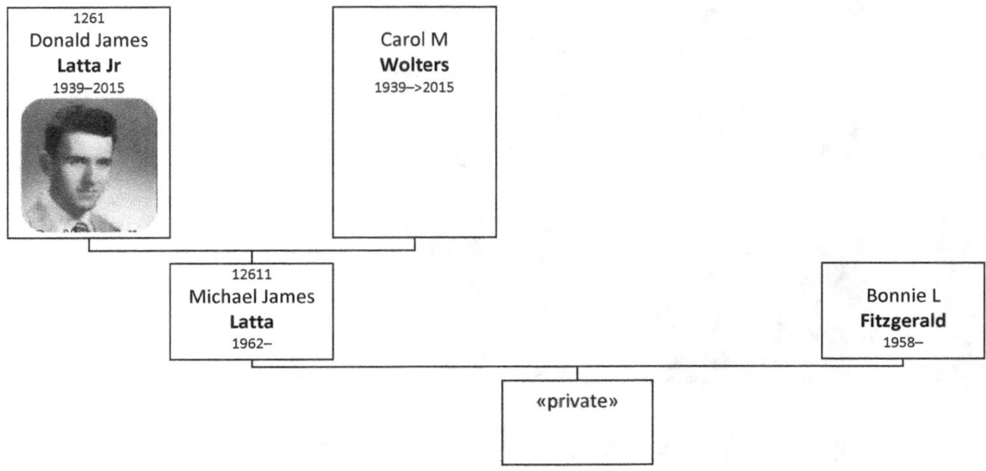

12611. **Michael James**[6] **Latta** was born on Thursday, June 21, 1962, in Lockport, Niagara, New York, USA.[90–92] He is the son of Donald James Latta Jr (1261) and Carol M Wolters.

More facts and events for Michael James Latta:

Residence: 1978   Lockport, Niagara, New York, USA[92]
                           Lockport High School

Residence: 1993 - 1995   Lockport, Niagara, New York, USA[91, 93]

Residence: 2000 - 2002   Lockport, Niagara, New York, USA[94]

Residence: Lockport, Niagara, New York, USA[90]

Residence: Lockport, Niagara, New York, USA[90]

They have one daughter: «private». Bonnie L Fitzgerald was born at (Likely) in Lockport, Niagara, New York, USA, on Wednesday, August 6, 1958.[90, 91]

More facts and events for Bonnie L Fitzgerald:

Residence: 1992   Lockport, Niagara, New York, USA[90, 91]

90   Ancestry.com, U.S. Public Records Index, Volume 2 (Provo, UT, USA, Ancestry.com Operations, Inc., 2010), Ancestry.com.

91   Ancestry.com, U.S. Public Records Index, Volume 1 (Provo, UT, USA, Ancestry.com Operations, Inc., 2010), Ancestry.com.

92   Ancestry.com, U.S. School Yearbooks (Provo, UT, USA, Ancestry.com Operations, Inc., 2010), Ancestry.com, "U.S., School Yearbooks, 1880-2012"; School Name: Lockport High School; Year: 1978.
     [Source citation includes one media item]

93   Ancestry.com, U.S. Phone and Address Directories, 1993-2002 (Provo, UT, USA, Ancestry.com Operations Inc, 2005), Ancestry.com, City: Lockport; State: New York; Year(s): 1993-1995.

94   Ancestry.com, U.S. Phone and Address Directories, 1993-2002 (Provo, UT, USA, Ancestry.com Operations Inc, 2005), Ancestry.com, City: Lockport; State: New York; Year(s): 2000-2002.

Figure 24: M Latta
"U.S., School Yearbooks, 1880-2012"; School Name:
Lockport High School; Year: 1978

Douglas Howe Latta

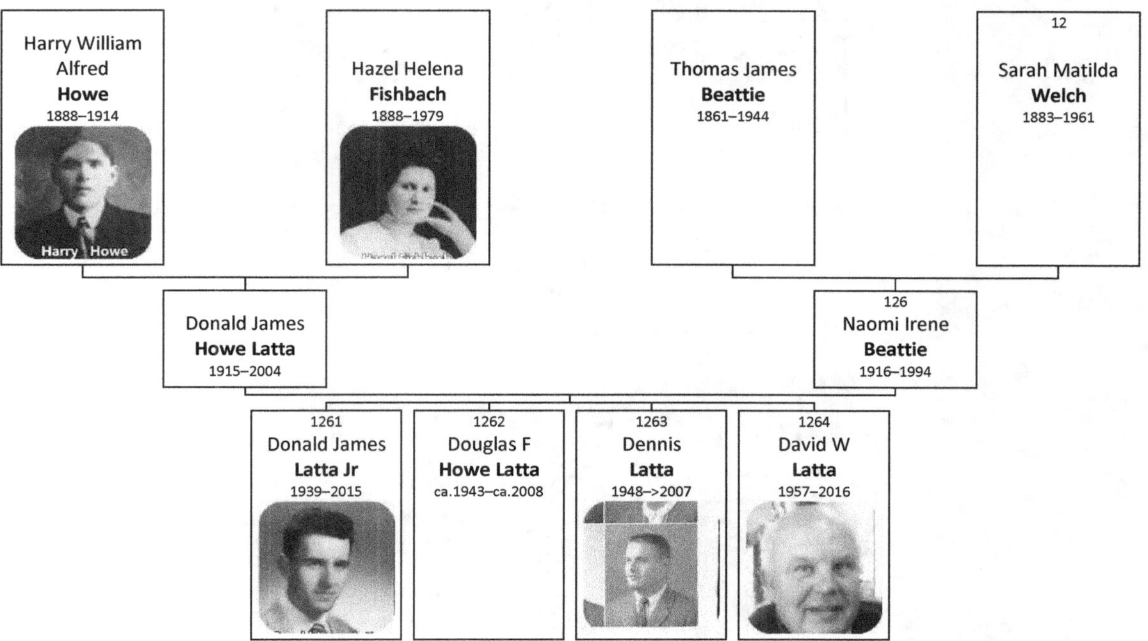

1262. **Douglas F[5] Howe Latta** was born about 1943 at (Likely) in Lockport, Niagara, New York, USA.[95, 96] He was the son of Donald James Howe Latta and Naomi Irene Beattie (126).

Douglas F died about 2008 at the age of 65.[96]

95   Ancestry.com, Web: Obituary Daily Times Index, 1995-2012 (Provo, UT, USA, Ancestry.com Operations, Inc., 2012), Ancestry.com.

96   Ancestry.com, Beta: Newspapers.com Obituary Index, 1940-1955 (Lehi, UT, USA, Ancestry.com Operations Inc, 2019), Ancestry.com, Star Tribune; Publication Date: 21/ Nov/ 2008; Publication Place: Minneapolis, Minnesota, United States of America; URL: https://www.newspapers.com/image/250709225/?article=cf448ce9-b27f-4f8c-8360-51eb388b177e&focus=0.34251535,0.7321204,0.4978047 6,0.763250.

South Suburban Evangelical Free
Church, 12600 Johnny Cake Ridge
Road, Apple Valley (952) 431-5466.
Private entombment, Lakewood
Mausoleum.

Howe, Douglas F.

age 65, of Blaine. Notice Sunday.
Methven-Taylor 763-786-2127
www.methven-taylor.com

Kroyer, Francis C. "Frank"

Age 73, of Shakopee. Sur-
vived by wife, Shirley;
daughters, Deb (Bob)

Figure 25: Obituary for Douglas F. Howe (Aged 65)
(November 21, 2008)

Family of Dennis Latta and Shirley Sharpe

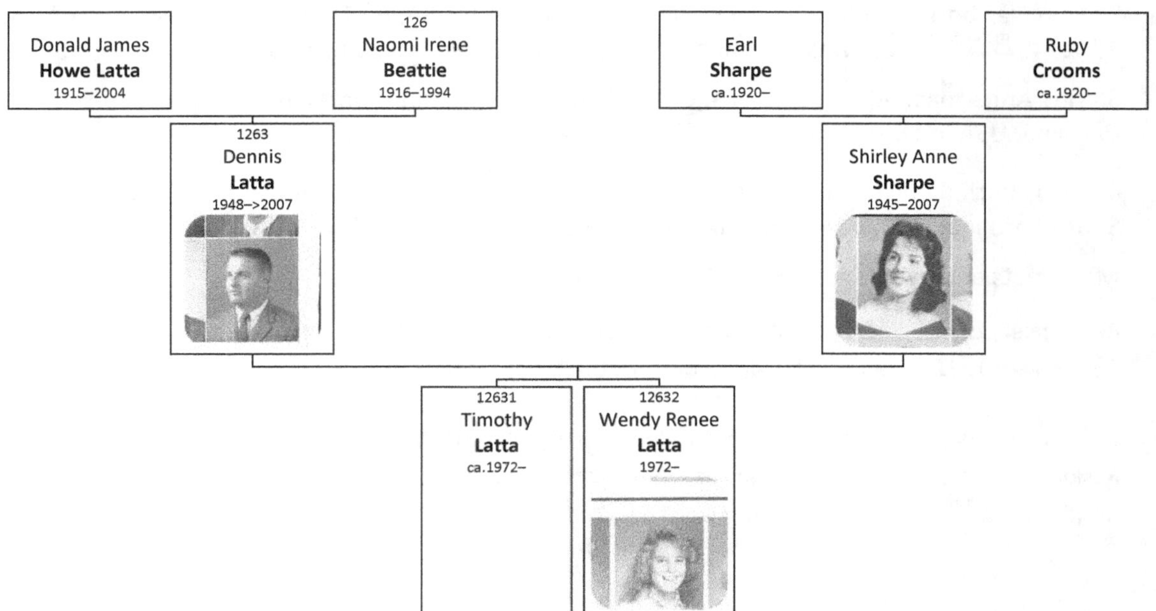

1263. **Dennis**[5] **Latta** was born on Thursday, August 19, 1948, at (Likely) in Lockport, Niagara, New York, USA.[97] He was the son of Donald James Howe Latta and Naomi Irene Beattie (126).

Dennis died after 2007.

Dennis Latta

More facts and events for Dennis Latta:

Residence: 1968   Columbia, Lexington, South Carolina, USA[98]
Residence: 1993   Mauldin, Greenville, South Carolina, USA[97]
Residence: 1995   Mauldin, Greenville, South Carolina, USA[97]

---

97   Ancestry.com, U.S. Public Records Index, Volume 1 (Provo, UT, USA, Ancestry.com Operations, Inc., 2010), Ancestry.com.

98   Ancestry.com, U.S. School Yearbooks (Provo, UT, USA, Ancestry.com Operations, Inc., 2010), Ancestry.com, "U.S., School Yearbooks, 1880-2012"; School Name: University of South Carolina; Year: 1968.
[Source citation includes one media item]

They had two children: Timothy (ca.1972–) and Wendy (1972–). Shirley Anne
Sharpe was born in Columbia, Richland, South Carolina, USA, on Thursday, January
25, 1945.[97, 99–104] She was the daughter of Earl Sharpe and Ruby Crooms.

Shirley Anne Sharpe

Shirley Anne reached 62 years of age and died in Fountain Inn, Greenville, South
Carolina, USA, on September 26, 2007.[99–101]

She was buried at Graceland East Memorial Park and Mausoleum, Simpsonville, Greenville County,
South Carolina, USA in Simpsonville, Greenville, South Carolina, USA.[100]

More facts and events for Shirley Anne Sharpe:

Residence: 1961   Charlotte, Mecklenburg, North Carolina, USA[103]

Residence: 1961   Taylorsville, Alexander, North Carolina, USA[102]
                   Taylorsville High School

Residence: 1962   Fountain Inn, Greenville, South Carolina, USA[101]

Residence: 1993   Mauldin, Greenville, South Carolina, USA[97]

Residence: Lexington, South Carolina, USA[104]

[99] Ancestry.com, Beta: Newspapers.com Obituary Index, 1940-1955 (Lehi, UT, USA, Ancestry.com Operations Inc, 2019), Ancestry.com, The
      Greenville News; Publication Date: 28/ Sep/ 2007; Publication Place: Greenville, South Carolina, United States of America; URL:
      https://www.newspapers.com/image/196269271/?article=a647ee9b-88d5-4cc3-ba5b-dbb62e49b5f4&focus=0.8308026,0.37056452,0.968665
      .

[100] Ancestry.com, U.S., Find A Grave Index, 1700s-Current (Provo, UT, USA, Ancestry.com Operations, Inc., 2012), Ancestry.com.

[101] Ancestry.com, U.S., Social Security Death Index, 1935-Current (Provo, UT, USA, Ancestry.com Operations Inc, 2011), Ancestry.com, Social
      Security Administration; Washington D.C., USA; Social Security Death Index, Master File.

[102] Ancestry.com, U.S. School Yearbooks (Provo, UT, USA, Ancestry.com Operations, Inc., 2010), Ancestry.com, "U.S., School Yearbooks,
      1880-2012"; School Name: Taylorsville High School; Year: 1961.
      [Source citation includes one media item]

[103] Ancestry.com, U.S. School Yearbooks (Provo, UT, USA, Ancestry.com Operations, Inc., 2010), Ancestry.com, "U.S., School Yearbooks,
      1880-2012"; School Name: East Mecklenburg High School; Year: 1961.
      [Source citation includes one media item]

[104] Ancestry.com, U.S. Public Records Index, Volume 2 (Provo, UT, USA, Ancestry.com Operations, Inc., 2010), Ancestry.com.

Shirley S. Latta
Fountain Inn

Shirley S. Latta, 62, of 2 James Jackson Drive, Fountain Inn, wife of Dennis Latta, died Wednesday, September 26, 2007.

Born in Columbia, S.C., she was a daughter of the late Earl Sharpe and Ruby Crooms Sharpe. Shirley was a homemaker and a member of the First Baptist Church of Mauldin.

Surviving are her husband, Dennis Latta of the home; a daughter, Wendy Fallow and her husband, Chris of Greer and a son, Tim Latta and his wife Stephanie of Simpsonville; and five grandchildren, Ashley, Blake, Lauren, Meghan and Katelyn.

The family will receive friends at The Mackey Mortuary, Century Drive, Saturday, September 29, 2007 from 10 to 11 a.m. Funeral services will follow at 11 a.m. in the Chapel with the Rev. Rick Wells officiating. Burial will be in Graceland East Memorial Park.

Messages of condolence may be sent to the family by visiting www.mackeymortuary.com.

Figure 26: Obituary for Shirley S . (Aged 62)
(September 28, 2007)

Family of Timothy Latta and Stepahnie ()

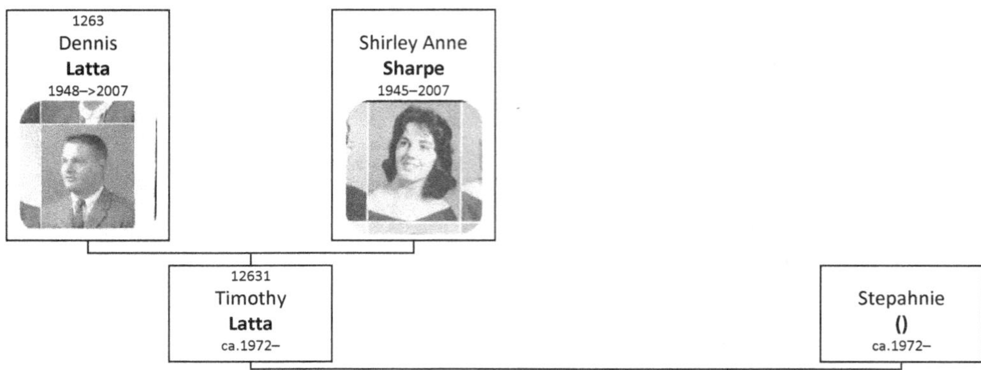

12631.   **Timothy**[6] **Latta** was born about 1972 at (Likely) in South Carolina, USA. He is the son of Dennis
         Latta (1263) and Shirley Anne Sharpe.

         More facts and events for Timothy Latta:

         Residence: September 26, 2007   Simpsonville, Greenville, South Carolina, USA
                                            Residence cited in mother's obituary.

         Stepahnie () was born at (Likely) in South Carolina, USA, about 1972.

Family of Wendy Latta and Christophe Fallow

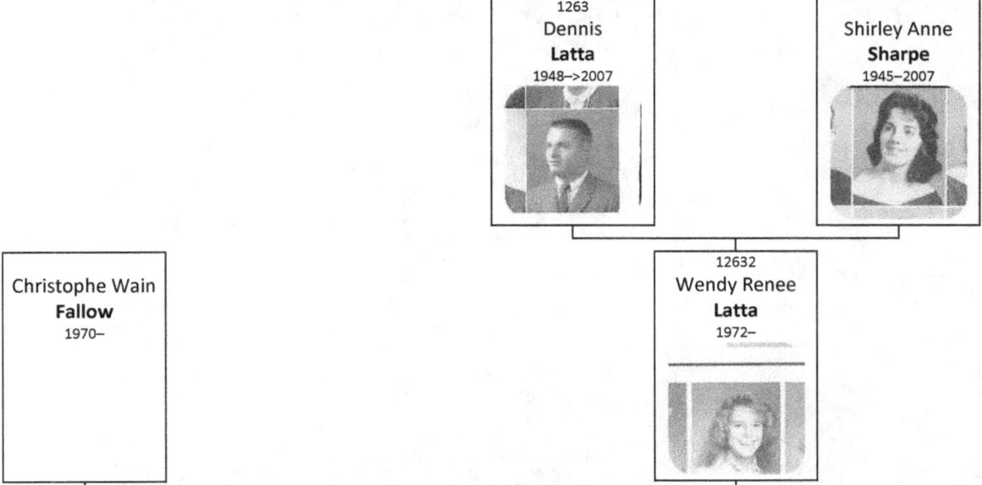

12632. **Wendy Renee[6] Latta** was born on Wednesday, May 24, 1972.[105, 106] She is the daughter of Dennis Latta (1263) and Shirley Anne Sharpe.

Wendy Renee Latta

More facts and events for Wendy Renee Latta:

Residence: 1988   Mauldin, Greenville, South Carolina, USA[106]
Mauldin High School

Residence: 1993   Mauldin, Greenville, South Carolina, USA[105]

Residence: September 26, 2007   Greer, Greenville, South Carolina, USA
Residence cited in mother's obituary.

Christophe Wain Fallow was born at (Likely) in New York, USA, on Saturday, December 19, 1970.[105, 107]

More facts and events for Christophe Wain Fallow:

Residence: 1995   Greenville, South Carolina, USA[105]

Residence: 1996   Greer, Greenville, South Carolina, USA[105]

Residence: Greer, Greenville, South Carolina, USA[107]

---

[105]   Ancestry.com, U.S. Public Records Index, Volume 1 (Provo, UT, USA, Ancestry.com Operations, Inc., 2010), Ancestry.com.

[106]   Ancestry.com, U.S. School Yearbooks (Provo, UT, USA, Ancestry.com Operations, Inc., 2010), Ancestry.com, "U.S., School Yearbooks, 1880-2012"; School Name: Mauldin High School; Year: 1988.
[Source citation includes one media item]

[107]   Ancestry.com, U.S. Public Records Index, Volume 2 (Provo, UT, USA, Ancestry.com Operations, Inc., 2010), Ancestry.com.

haffy of 317 W. Church Road, Easley. An Aug. 13 wedding is planned at St. Matthias Lutheran Church, Easley.

LATTA-FALLOW

MAULDIN — Mr. and Mrs. Dennis Wayne Latta of 202 Springvale Drive announce the engagement of their daughter, Wendy Renee Latta, to Christopher Wain Fallow, son of Mr. and Mrs. Wain Fallow of 11 Bransfield Road, Greenville. A summer 1995 wedding is planned.

LONG-STEVENS

GREENWOOD — Mr. and Mrs. Wheeler Thomas Long of 125 Donegal

Figure 27: Wedding Announcement
(June 26, 1994)

Family of David Latta and Mary McEachon

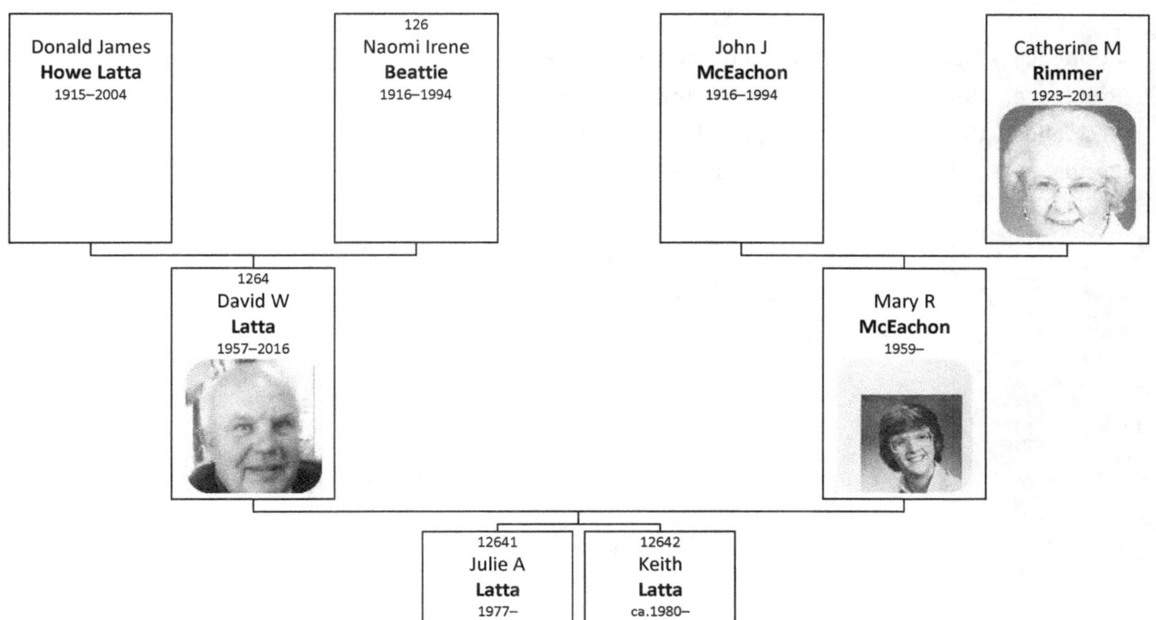

1264. **David W**[5] **Latta** was born on Tuesday, May 21, 1957, in Lockport, Niagara, New York, USA.[108–110] He was the son of Donald James Howe Latta and Naomi Irene Beattie (126).

David W died in Lockport, Niagara, New York, USA, on October 26, 2016, at the age of 59.[108, 109] He was buried at Cold Springs Cemetery, Lockport, Niagara County, New York, USA in Lockport, Niagara, New York, USA.[109]

David W Latta

More facts and events for David W Latta:

Residence: Lockport, Niagara, New York, USA[110]

They had two children: Julie (1977–) and Keith (ca.1980–). Mary R McEachon was born at (Likely) in Lockport, Niagara, New York, USA, on Wednesday, July 22, 1959.[110–112] She is the daughter of John J McEachon and Catherine M Rimmer.

Mary R McEachon

More facts and events for Mary R McEachon:

Residence: 1960   Lockport, Niagara, New York, USA[113]

---

108   Ancestry.com, U.S. Cemetery and Funeral Home Collection (Provo, UT, USA, Ancestry.com Operations Inc, 2011), Ancestry.com, Lange Funeral Home, Inc; Publication Place: Lockport, NY, US; URL: https://langefuneralhomeinc.com/tribute/details/425/David-Latta/obituary.html.

109   Ancestry.com, U.S., Find A Grave Index, 1700s-Current (Provo, UT, USA, Ancestry.com Operations, Inc., 2012), Ancestry.com.

110   Ancestry.com, U.S. Public Records Index, Volume 2 (Provo, UT, USA, Ancestry.com Operations, Inc., 2010), Ancestry.com.

111   Ancestry.com, U.S. Public Records Index, Volume 1 (Provo, UT, USA, Ancestry.com Operations, Inc., 2010), Ancestry.com.

112   Ancestry.com, U.S. School Yearbooks (Provo, UT, USA, Ancestry.com Operations, Inc., 2010), Ancestry.com, "U.S., School Yearbooks, 1880-2012"; School Name: Lockport High School; Year: 1977.
       [Source citation includes one media item]

Residence: 1977   Lockport, Niagara, New York, USA[112]
                    Lockport High School
Residence: 1986   Lockport, Niagara, New York, USA[111]
Residence: 1993   Lockport, Niagara, New York, USA[111]
Residence: 1996   Lockport, Niagara, New York, USA[111]
Residence: Lockport, Niagara, New York, USA[110, 111]

More figures:
Page 54, Figure 22: Cold Springs Cemetery

[113] Ancestry.com, U.S. City Directories, 1821-1989 (Provo, UT, USA, Ancestry.com Operations, Inc., 2011), Ancestry.com.
[Source citation includes one media item]

Family of Julie Latta and Steven Clement

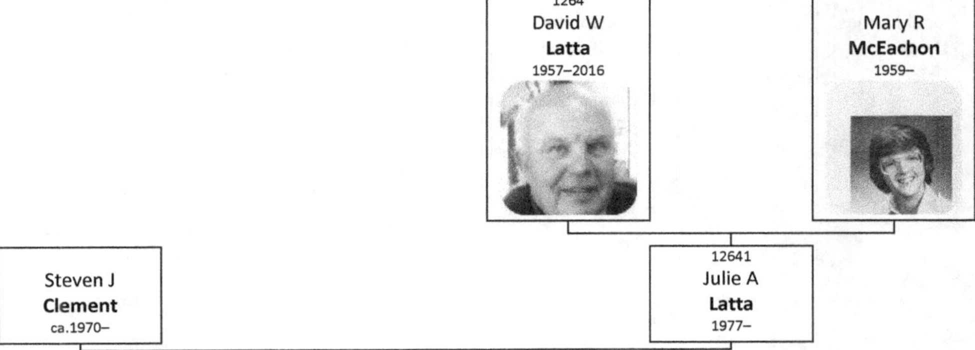

12641. **Julie A**[6] **Latta** was born on Thursday, June 30, 1977, at (Likely) in Lockport, Niagara, New York, USA.[114, 115] She is the daughter of David W Latta (1264) and Mary R McEachon.

More facts and events for Julie A Latta:

Residence: Lewis Center, Delaware, Ohio, USA[115]

Steven J Clement was born about 1970.[114]

---

114   Ancestry.com, Ohio Marriage Index, 1970, 1972-2007 (Provo, UT, Ancestry.com Operations, Inc, 2010), Ancestry.com, Ohio Department of Health; Columbus, Ohio; Ohio Marriage Index, 1970 and 1972-2007.

115   Ancestry.com, U.S. Public Records Index, Volume 2 (Provo, UT, USA, Ancestry.com Operations, Inc., 2010), Ancestry.com.

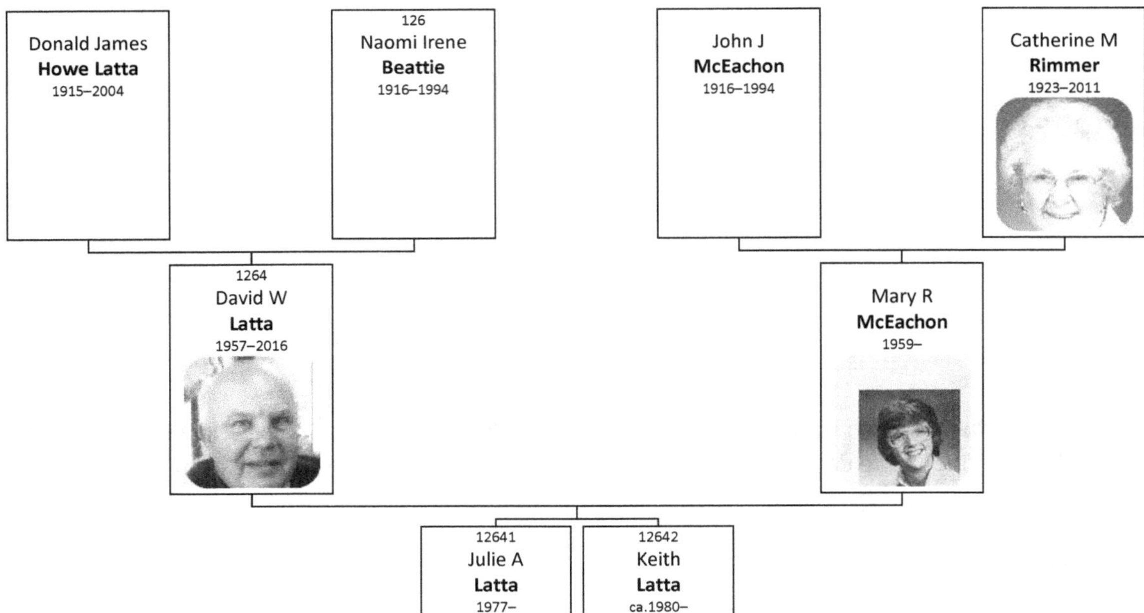

12642. **Keith**[6] **Latta** was born about 1980 at (Likely) in Lockport, Niagara, New York, USA. He is the son of David W Latta (1264) and Mary R McEachon.

Family of John Beattie and Mary Kyle

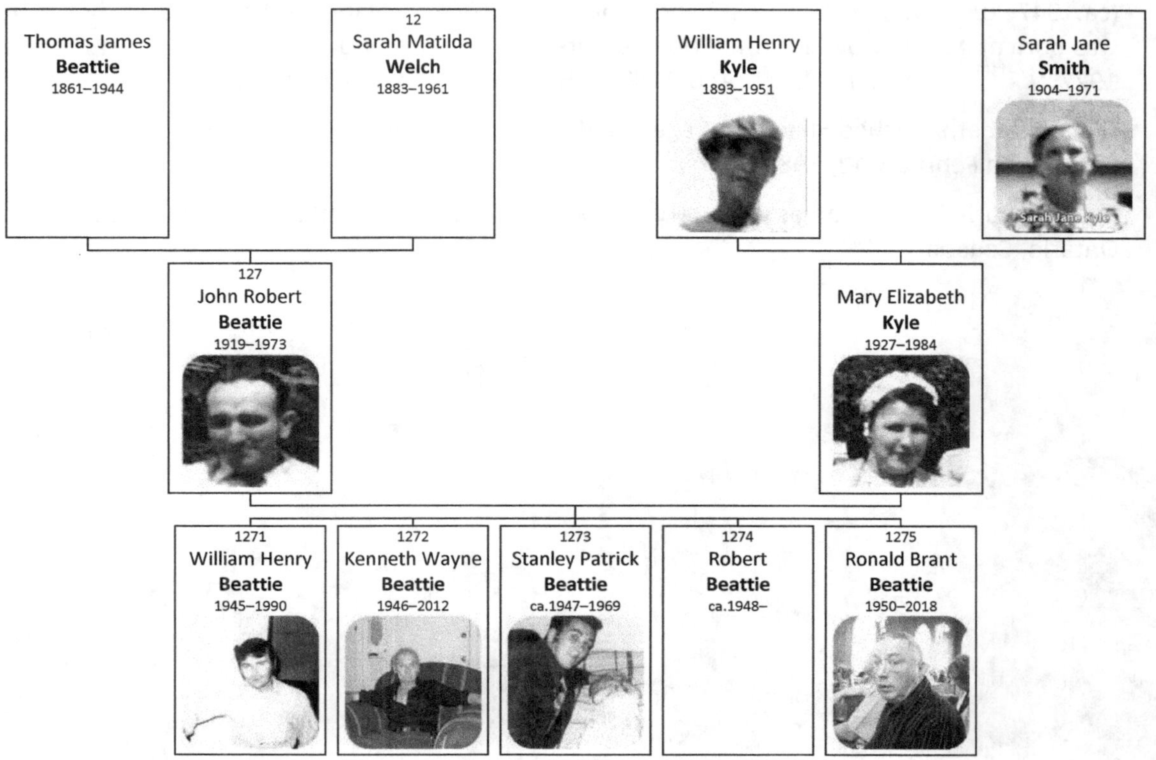

127. **John Robert[4] Beattie** was born in 1919 in St Thomas, Elgin, Ontario, Canada.[116–118] He was the son of Thomas James Beattie and Sarah Matilda Welch (12).

John Robert died in St Thomas, Elgin, Ontario, Canada, in 1973 at the age of 54.[117, 118] He was buried at Saint Thomas Cemetery, St. Thomas, Elgin County, Ontario, Canada in St Thomas, Elgin, Ontario, Canada.[117, 118]

John Robert Beattie

More facts and events for John Robert Beattie:

Residence: June 1, 1921   St Thomas, Elgin, Ontario, Canada[116]
Single; Son / Cohab: Thomas Beattie 62, Sarah Beattie 48, James Beattie 18, William Beattie 14, Viola Beattie 10, Lottie Beattie 8, Neoma Beattie 6, John Beattie 1.

Residence: 1944   St Thomas, Elgin, Ontario, Canada
Residence cited in father's obituary.

116   Ancestry.com, 1921 Census of Canada (Provo, UT, USA, Ancestry.com Operations Inc, 2013), Ancestry.com, Reference Number: RG 31; Folder Number: 55; Census Place: St Thomas (City), Elgin West, Ontario; Page Number: 22.
[Source citation includes one media item]

117   Ancestry.com, Canada, Find A Grave Index, 1600s-Current (Provo, UT, USA, Ancestry.com Operations, Inc., 2012), Ancestry.com.

118   Ancestry.com, Web: Canada, GenWeb Cemetery Index (Provo, UT, USA, Ancestry.com Operations, Inc., 2013), Ancestry.com.

They had five sons: William (1945–1990), Kenneth (1946–2012), Stanley (ca.1947–1969), Robert (ca.1948–) and Ronald (1950–2018). Mary Elizabeth Kyle was born at Aughnacloy in Tyrone, Northern Ireland, on Sunday, July 3, 1927.[117–119] She was the daughter of William Henry Kyle and Sarah Jane Smith.

Mary Elizabeth Kyle

Mary Elizabeth reached 56 years of age and died in St Thomas, Elgin, Ontario, Canada, on February 12, 1984.[117, 118]

She was buried at St Thomas Cemetery, St Thomas Elgin County Ontario Canada in St Thomas, Elgin, Ontario, Canada.[117, 118]

Figure 28: John Robert Beattie

Figure 29: Proud Grandparents
Mary holding Deb and Jack Beattie

[119]   Ancestry.com, Canadian Passenger Lists, 1865-1935 (Provo, UT, USA, Ancestry.com Operations Inc, 2010), Ancestry.com, Library and Archives Canada; Ottawa, Ontario, Canada; Series: RG 76-C; Roll: T-14855.
[Source citation includes one media item]

Figure 30: The Beattie Boys
(about 1950)

Figure 31: The Beattie Boys
(about 1952)
Robert, William, Kenneth, Stanley & Ronald Brant

Figure 32: Jack and Mary Beattie
(September 1960)

More figures:
Page 44, Figure 18: Saint Thomas West Avenue Cemetery

William Beattie

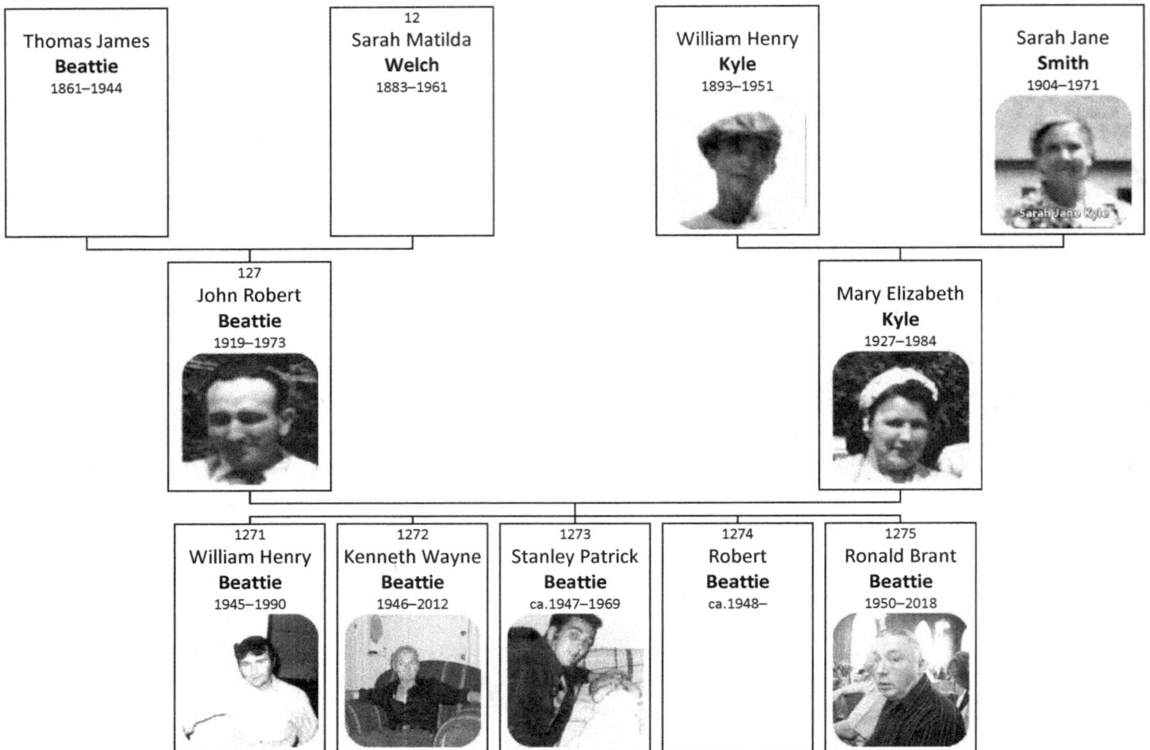

1271. **William Henry**[5] **Beattie** was born on Sunday, October 14, 1945, in St Thomas, Elgin, Ontario, Canada.[120] He was the son of John Robert Beattie (127) and Mary Elizabeth Kyle.

William Henry died in London, Middlesex, Ontario, Canada, on February 20, 1990, at the age of 44.[120] He was buried at Mount Pleasant Cemetery, Middlesex County, ON in London, Middlesex, Ontario, Canada.[120]

More facts and events for William Henry Beattie:

Residence: 1965   London, Middlesex, Ontario, Canada[121]
                    Occupation: Carpenter

William Henry Beattie

[120]   Ancestry.com, Web: Canada, GenWeb Cemetery Index (Provo, UT, USA, Ancestry.com Operations, Inc., 2013), Ancestry.com.

[121]   Ancestry.com, Canada, Voters Lists, 1935-1980 (Provo, UT, USA, Ancestry.com Operations, Inc., 2012), Ancestry.com, Library and Archives Canada; Ottawa, Ontario, Canada; Voters Lists, Federal Elections, 1935-1980.
        [Source citation includes one media item]

Figure 33: Mount Pleasant Cemetery and Crematorium

Figure 34: William Henry Beattie

Figure 35: William Henry Beattie Family
(about 1970)

More figures:
Page 71, Figure 30: The Beattie Boys
Page 71, Figure 31: The Beattie Boys

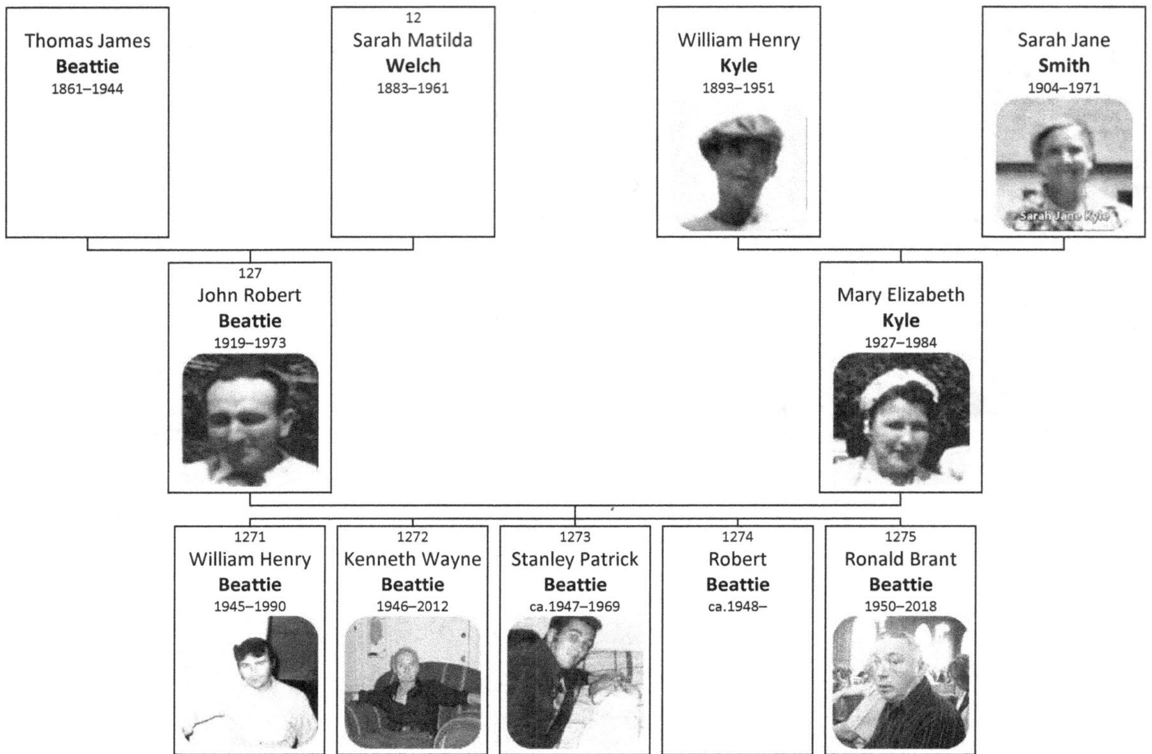

1272. **Kenneth Wayne**[5] **Beattie** was born on Monday, November 25, 1946, in St Thomas, Elgin, Ontario, Canada.[122] He was the son of John Robert Beattie (127) and Mary Elizabeth Kyle.

Kenneth Wayne died in London, Middlesex, Ontario, Canada, on January 22, 2012, at the age of 65.[122] He was buried in St Thomas, Elgin, Ontario, Canada.[122]

Kenneth Wayne
Beattie

---

122   Ancestry.com, Canada, Find A Grave Index, 1600s-Current (Provo, UT, USA, Ancestry.com Operations, Inc., 2012), Ancestry.com.

Figure 36: Kenneth Beattie
(about 1970)

More figures:
Page 71, Figure 30: The Beattie Boys
Page 71, Figure 31: The Beattie Boys

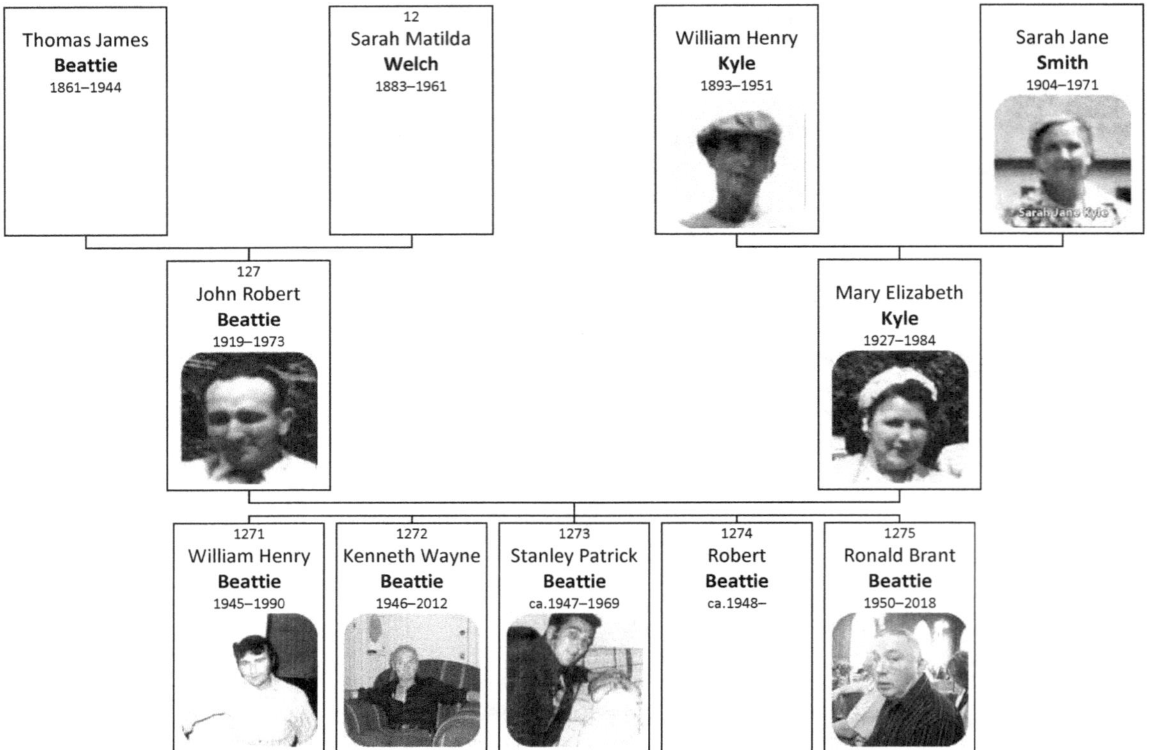

1273. **Stanley Patrick[5] Beattie** was born about 1947 in St Thomas, Elgin, Ontario, Canada. He was the son of John Robert Beattie (127) and Mary Elizabeth Kyle.

Stanley Patrick died in St Thomas, Elgin, Ontario, Canada, in 1969 at the age of 22.

Stanley Patrick Beattie

Figure 37: Billy Beattie
Billy Beattie with Brother Stanley in the background

More figures:
Page 71, Figure 30: The Beattie Boys

Page 71, Figure 31: The Beattie Boys

Page 71, Figure 31: The Beattie Boys

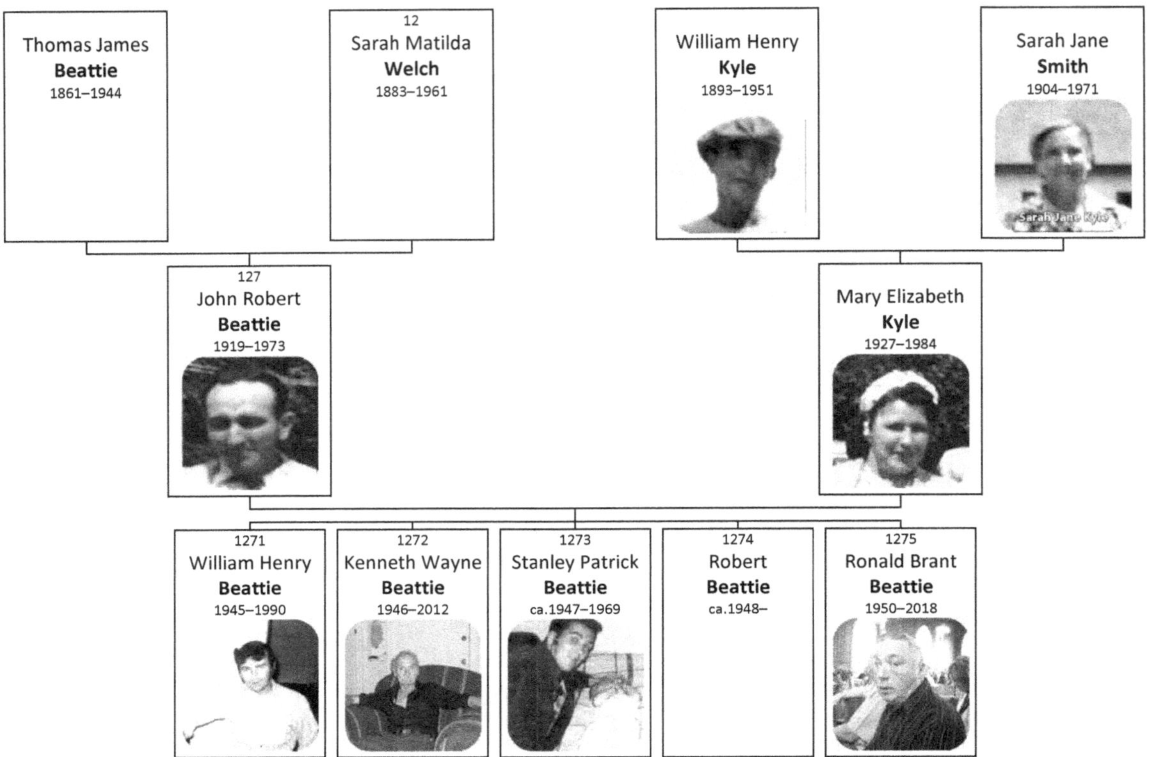

1274. **Robert**[5] **Beattie** was born about 1948 at (Likely) in Elgin, Ontario, Canada. He is the son of John Robert Beattie (127) and Mary Elizabeth Kyle.

More figures:
Page 71, Figure 30: The Beattie Boys
Page 71, Figure 31: The Beattie Boys

Ronald Beattie

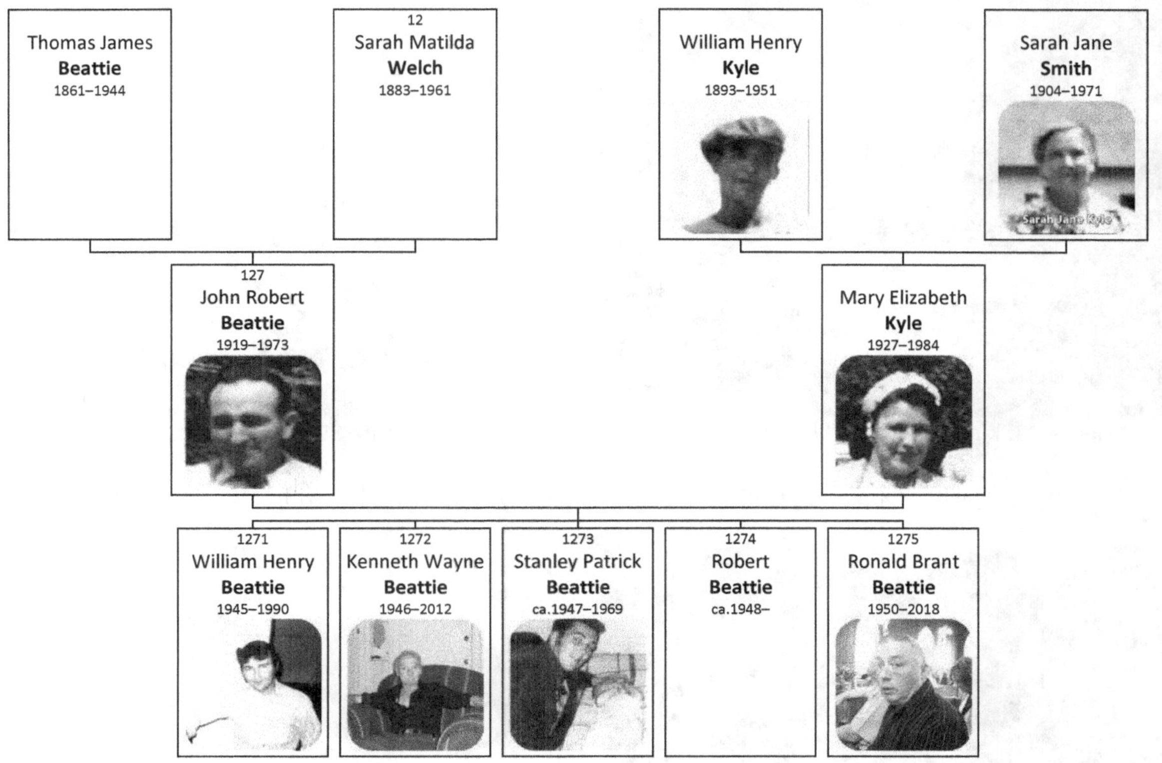

1275. **Ronald Brant[5] Beattie** was born on Saturday, April 15, 1950, in St Thomas, Elgin, Ontario, Canada. He was the son of John Robert Beattie (127) and Mary Elizabeth Kyle.

Ronald Brant Beattie

Ronald Brant died in New Hamburg, Waterloo, Ontario, Canada, on December 10, 2018, at the age of 68.

More facts and events for Ronald Brant Beattie:

Residence: 1962 Aylmer, Elgin, Ontario, Canada[123]
        Cohab: Ronald Beattie (Trucker); Mrs Ronald

Residence: 1965 Aylmer, Elgin, Ontario, Canada[123]
        Cohab: Ronald Beattie (Labourer); Mrs Ronald

Residence: 1995 - 2001 Aylmer, Elgin, Ontario, Canada[124]

123 Ancestry.com, Canada, Voters Lists, 1935-1980 (Provo, UT, USA, Ancestry.com Operations, Inc., 2012), Ancestry.com, Library and Archives Canada; Ottawa, Ontario, Canada; Voters Lists, Federal Elections, 1935-1980.
[Source citation includes one media item]

124 Ancestry.com, Canadian Phone and Address Directories, 1995-2002 (Provo, UT, USA, Ancestry.com Operations Inc, 2005), Ancestry.com.

Figure 38: Kim, Ronnie and Deb Cross
(April 2007)
First meeting with Ronnie at Debbie's

Figure 39: Ronald Brant Beattie
(April 28, 2007)
Ronald Brant Beattie with Uncle Joe.   First reunion visit.

Figure 40: Ronald Brant Beattie
(May 2007)
Ron at Home in St. Thomas

Figure 41: Uncle Joe and Ronnie
(May 27, 2007)
Anniversary Service in Iona

Figure 42: Ron Beattie with Uncle Joey
(June 2, 2007)
Waterworks Park Saturday afternoon visit

More figures:
Page 71, Figure 30: The Beattie Boys
Page 71, Figure 31: The Beattie Boys

Unnamed Beattie

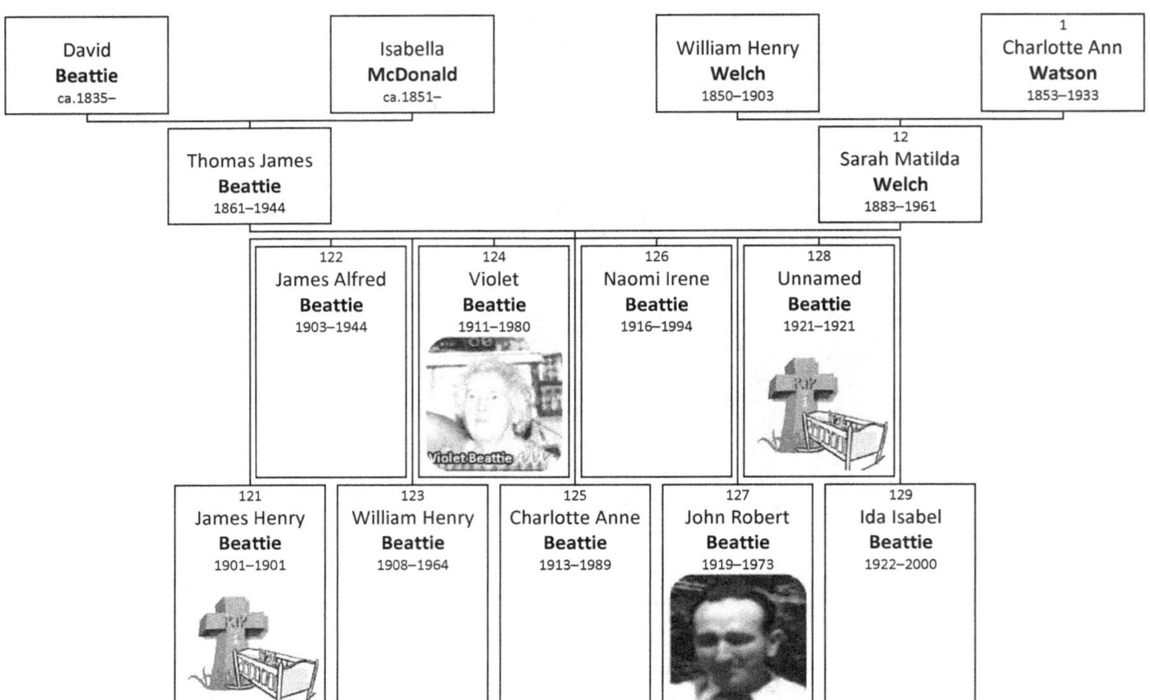

128. **Unnamed[4] Beattie** was born on Thursday, April 28, 1921, in St Thomas, Elgin, Ontario, Canada.[125] She was the daughter of Thomas James Beattie and Sarah Matilda Welch (12).

Unnamed died in St Thomas, Elgin, Ontario, Canada, on April 30, 1921.[125]

Unnamed Beattie

---

125   Ancestry.com, Ontario, Canada, Deaths, 1869-1938 and Deaths Overseas, 1939-1947 (Provo, UT, USA, Ancestry.com Operations Inc, 2010), Ancestry.com, Archives of Ontario; Toronto, Ontario, Canada; Series: MS935; Reel: 276.
[Source citation includes one media item]

Family of Ida Beattie and Kenneth Forbes

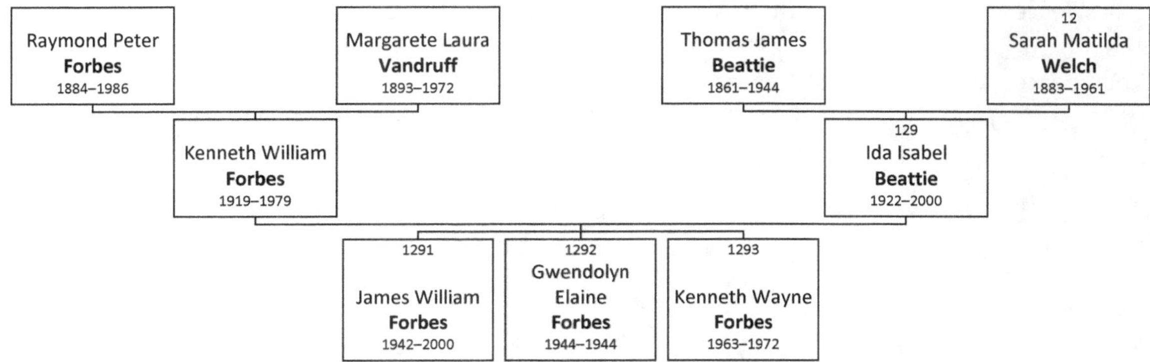

129.   **Ida Isabel[4] Beattie** was born in 1922 in St Thomas, Elgin, Ontario, Canada.[126, 127] She was the daughter of Thomas James Beattie and Sarah Matilda Welch (12).

Ida Isabel died in St Thomas, Elgin, Ontario, Canada, in 2000 at the age of 78.[126, 127] She was buried at Elmdale Memorial Park Cemetery, Section: E   190 Wilson Avenue , St Thomas, Yarmouth Township   Elgin County, ON in St Thomas, Elgin, Ontario, Canada.[126]

More facts and events for Ida Isabel Beattie:

Residence: 1962   St Thomas, Elgin, Ontario, Canada[128]
HH: Kenneth Forbes (labourer); Ida, John K (labourer)

Residence: 1972   St Thomas, Elgin, Ontario, Canada[128]
HH: Kenneth Forbes (retired); Mrs ida, Gary (attendant); Patricia (factory worker)

They had three children: James (1942–2000), Gwendolyn (1944–1944) and Kenneth (1963–1972). Kenneth William Forbes was born in Regina, Saskatchewan, Canada, on Wednesday, January 29, 1919.[129–131] He was the son of Raymond Peter Forbes and Margarete Laura Vandruff.

Kenneth William reached 59 years of age and died in St Thomas, Elgin, Ontario, Canada, in 1979.

More facts and events for Kenneth William Forbes:

Residence: June 1, 1921   Moose Jaw, Saskatchewan, Canada[129]
Single;   Son / OK Marquis Municipality 20-27-2   / HH: aymond Peter Forbes 37,   Peter Forbes 80,   Margarete Laura Forbes 28,   Eugene Forbes 5,   Kennith William Forbes 2,   Alice Edith Lyda Forbes 5m,   William John Anderson 27.

Residence: 1962   St Thomas, Elgin, Ontario, Canada[128]

126   Ancestry.com, Web: Canada, GenWeb Cemetery Index (Provo, UT, USA, Ancestry.com Operations, Inc., 2013), Ancestry.com.

127   Ancestry.com, Web: Obituary Daily Times Index, 1995-2012 (Provo, UT, USA, Ancestry.com Operations, Inc., 2012), Ancestry.com.

128   Ancestry.com, Canada, Voters Lists, 1935-1980 (Provo, UT, USA, Ancestry.com Operations, Inc., 2012), Ancestry.com, Library and Archives Canada; Ottawa, Ontario, Canada; Voters Lists, Federal Elections, 1935-1980.
[Source citation includes one media item]

129   Ancestry.com, 1921 Census of Canada (Provo, UT, USA, Ancestry.com Operations Inc, 2013), Ancestry.com, Reference Number: RG 31; Folder Number: 156; Census Place: Moose Jaw, Saskatchewan; Page Number: 10.
[Source citation includes one media item]

130   Ancestry.com, U.S., Social Security Applications and Claims Index, 1936-2007 (Provo, UT, USA, Ancestry.com Operations, Inc., 2015), Ancestry.com.

131   Ancestry.com, Michigan, Marriage Records, 1867-1952 (Provo, UT, USA, Ancestry.com Operations, Inc., 2015), Ancestry.com, Michigan Department of Community Health, Division of Vital Records and Health Statistics; Lansing, MI, USA; Michigan, Marriage Records, 1867-1952; Film: 341; Film Title: 82 Wayne 361100-364379; Film Description: Wayne (Dates TBD).

HH: Kenneth Forbes (labourer); Ida, John K (labourer)

Residence: 1963   St Thomas, Elgin, Ontario, Canada[128]

HH: Kenneth Forbes (groom)

Residence: 1972   St Thomas, Elgin, Ontario, Canada[128]

HH: Kenneth Forbes (retired); Mrs ida, Gary (attendant); Patricia (factory worker)

Figure 43: elmdale-st thomas

Tobacco in Elgin County

Tobacco was big business in Elgin County. A part of the tobacco belt, Elgin County tobacco farms contributed to the billions of pounds of tobacco that were produced in Ontario. Tobacco production was a major economic driver in the region and provided employment and income for hundreds of workers and farmers in the area. At its peak, Ontario tobacco producers grew over 200 million pounds of tobacco a year. However, taxation, increased importation and illegal contraband tobacco have contributed to the demise of a once thriving agricultural sector.

Tobacco started to be produced commercially around 1800. After 1854, U.S. tobacco was allowed to enter Canada duty-free and production in Ontario virtually ceased. When production in the tobacco belt in the U.S. was interrupted, as during the U.S. Civil War, tobacco production in Southwestern Ontario would increase, falling as U.S. production resumed regular levels.

Air-cured tobacco production began in 1800 in the counties of Essex and Kent. Flue-cured tobacco started being produced in these regions in 1958 and due to the potential for large profits it attracted growers from the USA, Europe and all over the world. The production of flue-cured tobacco started in Elgin County around 1925. After the Second World War many immigrants came to the area to farm tobacco. This made the once worthless sand land some of the most valuable real estate in the area. A general farm would sell for about $10,000 for 100 acres and a fully equipped farm of similar size would sell for $50,000.

1957: Ontario Flue-Cured Tobacco Growers' Marketing Board

Sanctioned by the Government under the Ontario Farm Products Marketing Act, the Ontario Flue-Cured Tobacco Growers' Marketing Board (the Marketing Board) was established in 1957 to replace the troublesome Ontario Flue-Cured Tobacco Growers' Marketing Association. It was initially made up of one representative each from 14 different district committees. The Marketing Board issued quota, known as Basic Market Acreage (BMA), to producers in order to control the production in order to meet the demand. This demand and also the base price were negotiated with the buyers by the Marketing Board. The tobacco would then be sold to buyers at a Marketing Board controlled auction warehouse. Three of these were built, one each in Delhi, Tillsonburg and Aylmer.

Auction Exchange

The auction market would start in November after the harvest of the tobacco. Bales are sent to the auction exchange warehouse and leaves from each bale are pulled for inspection by the buyers. The bales are then put on pallets and weighed. Once a weight has been assigned, a weigh ticket is issued and attached to the pallet and the bales. The weigh ticket contains the farm number, the serial number of the pallet, the weight of the pallet and the number of bales. The farm number is removed from the pallet and sent to the office in order to ensure anonymity during the auction. Next, the pallet is graded by licensed graders hired by the Marketing Board and checked by government graders.

Imperial Tobacco Plant, Aylmer

Imperial Tobacco opened their Aylmer plant in October of 1946. Imperial had two other plants in Leamington and Delhi, but Leamington was outdated and Delhi had run out of room to expand. The would eventually take up 55 acres, 21.5 of them under roof. In its prime, the plant could store 119 million tons of tobacco and had an October to April production capacity of 100 million tons. Of this, 20 to 25 million tons were for export to other countries, making it one of Canada's leading exporters. The rest of the processed tobacco would be shipped to Imperial's cigarette production plant in Guelph.

The plant was one of the largest employers in Aylmer and the surrounding area and at one point the plant had almost 600 employees. This consisted of 88 full-time staff who would take care of basic operations year round and 515 seasonal workers who would be hired on during the October to April processing season.

Tobacco's Demise

Family farms began to disappear in the 1970s and 1980s to be replaced with large commercial tobacco producers and demand for tobacco found itself in a steady decline as health concerns began to dominate government policy. During the 1980s, a combination of weather and disease coupled with historically high interest rates caused many to experience financial hardship. In 1979, blue mould destroyed nearly half of Ontario's tobacco crop. Three years later, in 1982, an early frost devastated many crops. These two events forced many farmers to refinance their mortgages or seek loans to fund the next year's planting of crops. These loans were at drastically high interest rates of 20%+ and forced many tobacco farmers out of business. Added to this financial hardship was the unpredictability of future tobacco demand which devalued the worth of these farms.

Source: St. Thomas – "Tobacco in Elgin County". Elgin County Archives

Figure 44: Tobacco in Elgin
(1957)

Figure 45: Kenneth and Ida Isabel (nee Beattie) Forbes
Gravestone
(August 2008)
Elmdale Memorial Park Cemetery, St Thomas, Yarmouth
Township, Elgin, Ontario, Canada. Inscription: KENNETH
(FLASH) / 1917-1979 / IDA ISABEL / 1922-2000 /
FORBES / TOGETHER FOREVER / UNTIL WE MEET AGAIN
{Photo courtesy of Darlene Ethel Elenor (nee
McCann-Ballantyne) Bateman}

James Forbes

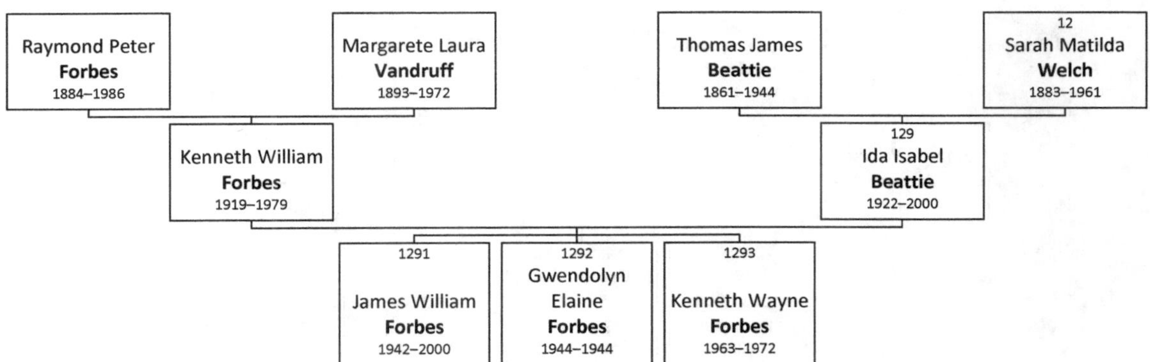

1291.   **James William[5] Forbes** was born on Tuesday, August 25, 1942, in St Thomas, Elgin, Ontario, Canada.[132, 133] He was the son of Kenneth William Forbes and Ida Isabel Beattie (129).

James William died in St Thomas, Elgin, Ontario, Canada, on April 25, 2000, at the age of 57.[132, 133] He was buried in St Thomas, Elgin, Ontario, Canada.[132]

132   Ancestry.com, Web: Canada, GenWeb Cemetery Index (Provo, UT, USA, Ancestry.com Operations, Inc., 2013), Ancestry.com.

133   Ancestry.com, Web: Obituary Daily Times Index, 1995-2012 (Provo, UT, USA, Ancestry.com Operations, Inc., 2012), Ancestry.com.

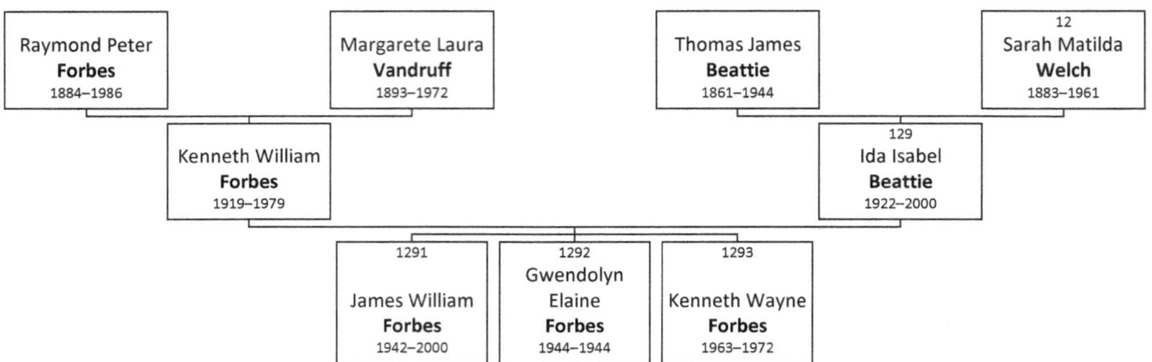

1292. **Gwendolyn Elaine[5] Forbes** was born on Friday, October 27, 1944, in St Thomas, Elgin, Ontario, Canada.[134] She was the daughter of Kenneth William Forbes and Ida Isabel Beattie (129).

Gwendolyn Elaine died in St Thomas, Elgin, Ontario, Canada, on October 30, 1944.[134]

---

134   Ancestry.com, Ontario, Canada, Deaths, 1869-1938 and Deaths Overseas, 1939-1947 (Provo, UT, USA, Ancestry.com Operations Inc, 2010), Ancestry.com, Archives of Ontario; Toronto, Ontario, Canada; Registrations of Deaths, 1944; Collection: Registrations of Deaths, 1944. [Source citation includes one media item]

Kenneth Forbes

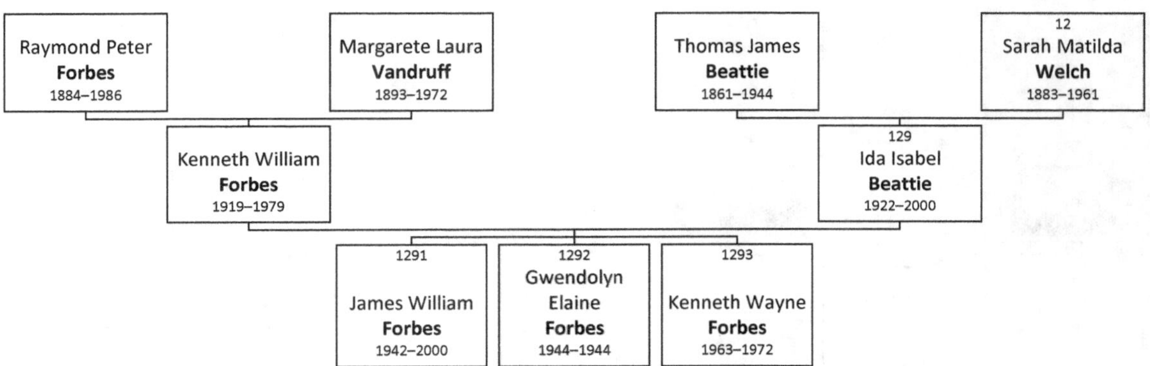

1293. **Kenneth Wayne[5] Forbes** was born in 1963. He was the son of Kenneth William Forbes and Ida Isabel Beattie (129).

Kenneth Wayne died in Elgin, Ontario, Canada, in 1972 at the age of 9.

Family of Neoma Welch and Robert Mills

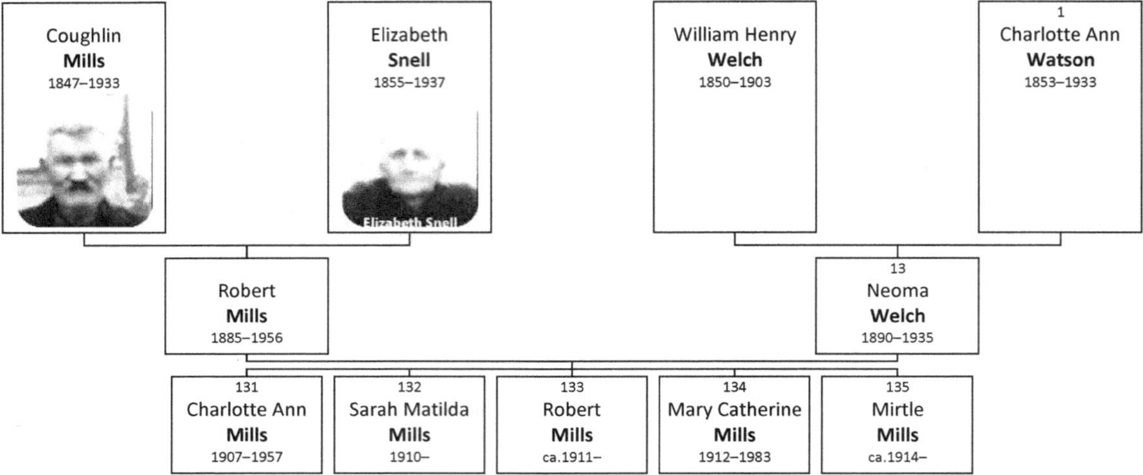

13.   **Neoma**[3] **Welch** was born in April 1890 at Southwold in Elgin, Ontario, Canada.[135–138] She was the daughter of William Henry Welch and Charlotte Ann Watson (1).

Neoma died at Died of double pneumonia and flu in Elgin, Ontario, Canada, on February 25, 1935, at the age of 44.[135, 136] She was buried at Evergreen / West Lorne Cemetery, Elgin County, ON in West Lorne, Elgin, Ontario, Canada.[136]

More facts and events for Neoma Welch:

Residence: 1911   West Lorne, Elgin, Ontario, Canada[137]
                          Married; Wife / Cohab: Robert Mills 25,   Reoma Mills 21,   Charlotte Ann Mills 3,
                          Sarah Matilda Mills 1.

Residence: June 1, 1921 West Lorne, Elgin, Ontario, Canada[138]
                          Baptist; Married;   Wife/ Cohab: Robert Mills 36, Neoma Mills 28, Lotty Mills 13,
                          Motile Mills 11, Robert Mills 10, Mirtle Mills 7, Mary Mills 8/12.

They had five children: Charlotte (1907–1957), Sarah (1910–), Robert (ca.1911–), Mary (1912–1983) and Mirtle (ca.1914–). Robert Mills was born at Aldborough in Elgin, Ontario, Canada, on Tuesday, June 16, 1885.[136–140] He was the son of Coughlin Mills and Elizabeth Snell.

---

135   Ancestry.com, Ontario, Canada, Deaths, 1869-1938 and Deaths Overseas, 1939-1947 (Provo, UT, USA, Ancestry.com Operations Inc, 2010), Ancestry.com, Archives of Ontario; Toronto, Ontario, Canada; Collection: MS935; Reel: 508.
       [Source citation includes one media item]

136   Ancestry.com, Web: Canada, GenWeb Cemetery Index (Provo, UT, USA, Ancestry.com Operations, Inc., 2013), Ancestry.com.

137   Ancestry.com, 1911 Census of Canada (Provo, UT, USA, Ancestry.com Operations Inc, 2006), Ancestry.com, Year: 1911; Census Place: 41 - West Lorne, Elgin West, Ontario; Page: 8; Family No: 100.
       [Source citation includes one media item]

138   Ancestry.com, 1921 Census of Canada (Provo, UT, USA, Ancestry.com Operations Inc, 2013), Ancestry.com, Reference Number: RG 31; Folder Number: 56; Census Place: 56, Elgin West, Ontario; Page Number: 2.
       [Source citation includes one media item]

139   Ancestry.com, 1891 Census of Canada (Provo, UT, USA, Ancestry.com Operations Inc, 2008), Ancestry.com, Year: 1891; Census Place: Aldborough, Elgin West, Ontario, Canada; Roll: T-6334; Family No: 143.
       [Source citation includes one media item]

140   Ancestry.com, 1901 Census of Canada (Provo, UT, USA, Ancestry.com Operations Inc, 2006), Ancestry.com, Year: 1901; Census Place: Aldborough, Elgin (West/Ouest), Ontario; Page: 1; Family No: 8.
       [Source citation includes one media item]

Robert reached 70 years of age and died at Aldborough in Elgin, Ontario, Canada, in 1956.[136] He was buried at Evergreen / West Lorne Cemetery, Elgin County, ON in West Lorne, Elgin, Ontario, Canada.[136]

More facts and events for Robert Mills:

Residence:	1891	Elgin, Ontario, Canada[139]
		Single; Son / Cohab: Lizzie Mills 35, John Mills 16, George Mills 13, William Mills 11, Emma Mills 9, Robert Mills 6, Henry Mills 4, Arther Mills 2.
Residence:	1901	Elgin, Ontario, Canada[140]
		Single; Son / Cohab: Coughleis Mills 48. Elisabeth Mills 44. Robert Mills 15. Arthur Mills 12. Sarah Mills 9.
Residence:	1911	West Lorne, Elgin, Ontario, Canada[137]
		Married; Head / Cohab: Robert Mills 25, Reoma Mills 21, Charlotte Ann Mills 3, Sarah Matilda Mills 1.
Residence:	June 1, 1921	West Lorne, Elgin, Ontario, Canada[138]
		Baptist; Married; Head; Labourer / Cohab: Robert Mills 36, Neoma Mills 28, Lotty Mills 13, Motile Mills 11, Robert Mills 10, Mirtle Mills 7, Mary Mills 8/12.
Residence:	1940	West Lorne, Elgin, Ontario, Canada[141]
		Robert Mills (Labourer)
Residence:	1953	West Lorne, Elgin, Ontario, Canada[141]
		Robert Mills (farmer)

Figure 46: Evergreen Cemetery-West Lorne

Figure 47: Robert Mills

---

[141]   Ancestry.com, Canada, Voters Lists, 1935-1980 (Provo, UT, USA, Ancestry.com Operations, Inc., 2012), Ancestry.com, Library and Archives Canada; Ottawa, Ontario, Canada; Voters Lists, Federal Elections, 1935-1980.
[Source citation includes one media item]

Family of Charlotte Mills and Gordon Campbell Pusey

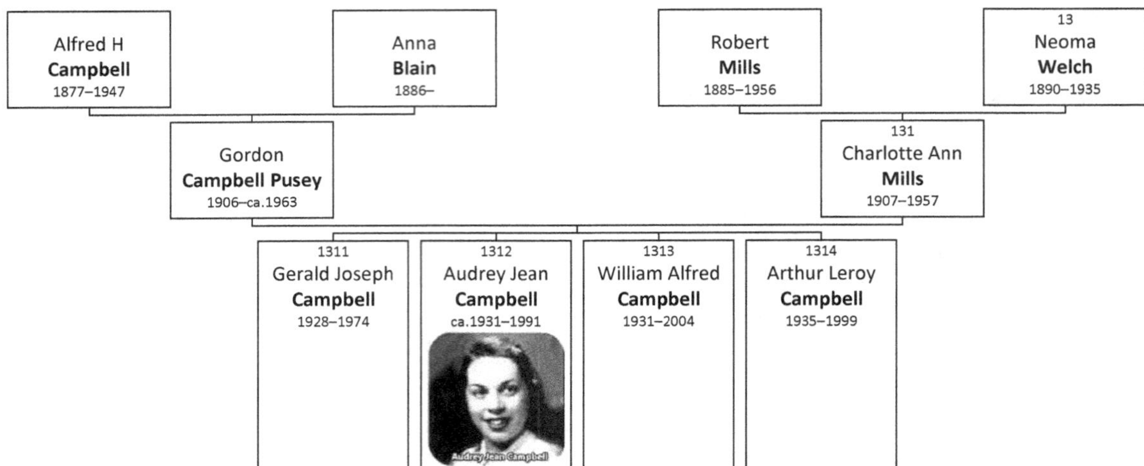

131. **Charlotte Ann[4] Mills** was born on Wednesday, December 25, 1907, in West Lorne, Elgin, Ontario, Canada.[142–146] She was the daughter of Robert Mills and Neoma Welch (13).

Charlotte Ann died in West Lorne, Elgin, Ontario, Canada, in 1957 at the age of 49.[146] She was buried at Evergreen Cemetery,   West Lorne, Elgin County, Ontario, Canada in West Lorne, Elgin, Ontario, Canada.[146]

More facts and events for Charlotte Ann Mills:

Residence: 1911   West Lorne, Elgin, Ontario, Canada[142]
                         Single; Dau / Cohab: Robert Mills 25,   Reoma Mills 21,   Charlotte Ann Mills 3,
                         Sarah Matilda Mills 1.
Residence: June 1, 1921   West Lorne, Elgin, Ontario, Canada[145]
                         Baptist; Single;   Dau / HH: Robert Mills 36,   Neoma Mills 28,   Lotty Mills 13,
                         Motile Mills 11,   Robert Mills 10,   Mirtle Mills 7,   Mary Mills 8/12.

They had four children: Gerald (1928–1974), Audrey (ca.1931–1991), William (1931–2004) and Arthur (1935–1999). Gordon Campbell Pusey was born at Brockville (illegitimate to Alfred Campbell and Anna Blain) in Leeds, Ontario, Canada, on Thursday, March 22, 1906.[144, 147–149] He was the son

---

[142]   Ancestry.com, 1911 Census of Canada (Provo, UT, USA, Ancestry.com Operations Inc, 2006), Ancestry.com, Year: 1911; Census Place: 41 - West Lorne, Elgin West, Ontario; Page: 8; Family No: 100.
[Source citation includes one media item]

[143]   Ancestry.com, Ontario, Canada Births, 1869-1913 (Provo, UT, USA, Ancestry.com Operations Inc, 2010), Ancestry.com, Archives of Ontario; Toronto, Ontario, Canada; Registrations of Births and Stillbirths, 1869-1913; Series: MS929; Reel: 4; Record Group: RG 80-2.
[Source citation includes one media item]

[144]   Ancestry.com and Genealogical Research Library (Brampton, Ontario, Canada), Ontario, Canada, Marriages, 1801-1928 (Provo, UT, USA, Ancestry.com Operations, Inc., 2010), Ancestry.com, Archives of Ontario; Toronto, Ontario, Canada; Registrations of Marriages, 1869-1928; Reel: 757.
[Source citation includes one media item]

[145]   Ancestry.com, 1921 Census of Canada (Provo, UT, USA, Ancestry.com Operations Inc, 2013), Ancestry.com, Reference Number: RG 31; Folder Number: 56; Census Place: 56, Elgin West, Ontario; Page Number: 2.
[Source citation includes one media item]

[146]   Ancestry.com, Canada, Find A Grave Index, 1600s-Current (Provo, UT, USA, Ancestry.com Operations, Inc., 2012), Ancestry.com.

[147]   Ancestry.com, 1911 Census of Canada (Provo, UT, USA, Ancestry.com Operations Inc, 2006), Ancestry.com, Year: 1911; Census Place: 27 - Sydenham, Grey North, Ontario; Page: 5; Family No: 45.
[Source citation includes one media item]

of Alfred H Campbell and Anna Blain. Gordon was adopted at Adopted by Alfred & Anna Pusey 2 yrs before Dolly (Maria Pusey's child) from same community in Grey, Ontario, Canada, about 1907.

Gordon reached 56 years of age and died in Toronto, Ontario, Canada, about 1963.

More facts and events for Gordon Campbell Pusey:

Residence: 1911   Grey, Ontario, Canada[147]
Single; Stepson   / HH: Alfred Pusey 47,   Ann Pusey 49,   Dorothy Pusey 17, Gordon Campbell 5.

Residence: June 1, 1921   Grey, Ontario, Canada[149]
Protestant; Single; Son / HH: Alfred Pusey 57, Ann Pusey 61, Gordon Pusey 15.

Residence: 1957   Meaford, Grey, Ontario, Canada[150]
HH: Gordon Campbell (gentleman)

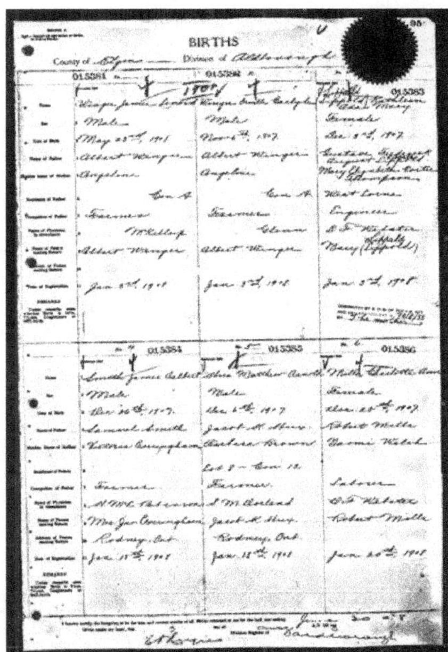

Figure 48: Mills, Charlotte Ann 1907
(2018-11-29 1:26:20 PM)
LEAD Technologies Inc. V1.01

More figures:
Page 89, Figure 46: Evergreen Cemetery-West Lorne

---

[148]   Ancestry.com, Ontario, Canada Births, 1869-1913 (Provo, UT, USA, Ancestry.com Operations Inc, 2010), Ancestry.com, Archives of Ontario; Toronto, Ontario, Canada; Registrations of Births and Stillbirths, 1869-1913; Series: MS929; Reel: 180; Record Group: RG 80-2.
[Source citation includes one media item]

[149]   Ancestry.com, 1921 Census of Canada (Provo, UT, USA, Ancestry.com Operations Inc, 2013), Ancestry.com, Reference Number: RG 31; Folder Number: 60; Census Place: 60, Grey North, Ontario; Page Number: 7.
[Source citation includes one media item]

[150]   Ancestry.com, Canada, Voters Lists, 1935-1980 (Provo, UT, USA, Ancestry.com Operations, Inc., 2012), Ancestry.com, Library and Archives Canada; Ottawa, Ontario, Canada; Voters Lists, Federal Elections, 1935-1980.
[Source citation includes one media item]

Family of Gerald Campbell and Linda ()

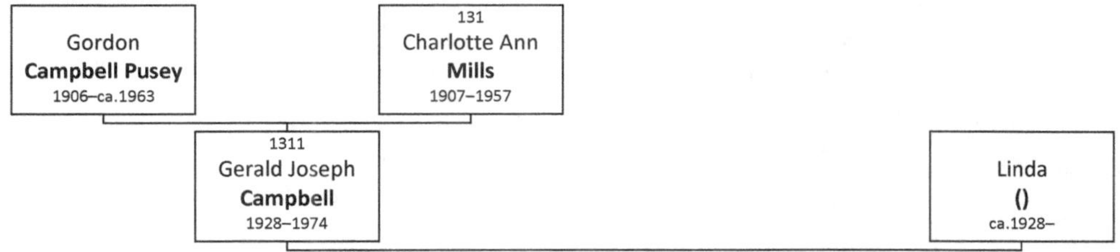

1311. **Gerald Joseph[5] Campbell** was born on Friday, September 21, 1928.[151] He was the son of Gordon Campbell Pusey and Charlotte Ann Mills (131).

Gerald Joseph died at (Likely) in Toronto, Ontario, Canada, on September 3, 1974, at the age of 45.[151] He was buried at 375 Mount Pleasant Road   Toronto, Toronto Municipality, Ontario, M4T 2V8 Canada in Toronto, Ontario, Canada.[152]

Linda () was born at (Likely) in Ontario, Canada, about 1928.

Figure 49: Gerald Joseph Campbell

Figure 50: Mount Pleasant Cemetery-Toronto

151   Ancestry.com, International, Find A Grave Index for Select Locations, 1300s-Current (Provo, UT, USA, Ancestry.com Operations, Inc., 2012), Ancestry.com.

152   Ancestry.com, Web: CanadianHeadstones.com Index (Provo, UT, USA, Ancestry.com Operations, Inc., 2012), Ancestry.com, Canadian Headstones; Canada.

Family of Audrey Campbell and Harold Seaton

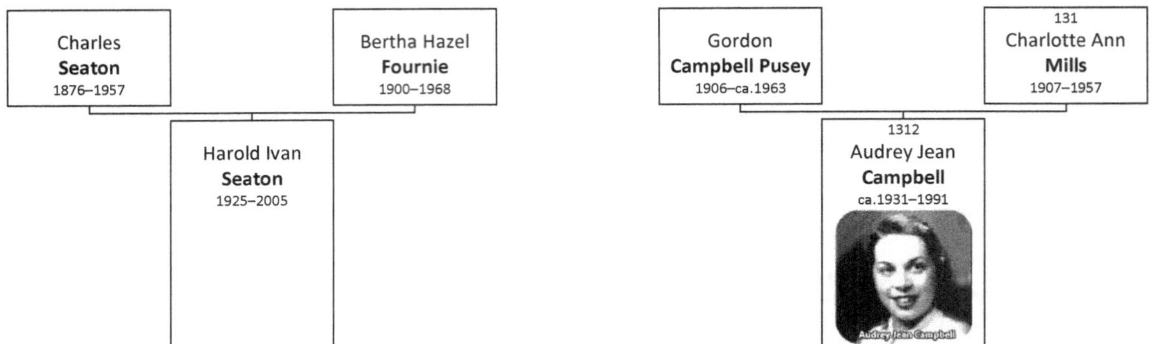

1312. **Audrey Jean**[5] **Campbell** was born about 1931 in Ontario, Canada.[153] She was the daughter of Gordon Campbell Pusey and Charlotte Ann Mills (131).

Audrey Jean died at Brussels in Huron, Ontario, Canada, on September 19, 1991, at the age of 60.[154] She was buried at Brussels in Huron, Ontario, Canada.[154]

Audrey Jean Campbell

More facts and events for Audrey Jean Campbell:

Residence: 1951   London, Middlesex, Ontario, Canada[153]
                 London Normal School

Residence: 1957   Chatham-Kent, Kent, Ontario, Canada[155]
                 HH: Harold Seaton (labourer); Audrey

Residence: 1963   Chatham-Kent, Kent, Ontario, Canada[155]
                 HH: Harold Campbell (Garage operator); Audrey (stenographer)

Residence: 1974   Chatham-Kent, Kent, Ontario, Canada[155]
                 HH: Harold Campbell (garage operator); Mrs Audrey (secretary)

Harold Ivan Seaton was born in Chatham-Kent, Kent, Ontario, Canada, on Tuesday, May 5, 1925. He was the son of Charles Seaton and Bertha Hazel Fournie.

Harold Ivan reached 79 years of age and died in Chatham-Kent, Kent, Ontario, Canada, in 2005.

More facts and events for Harold Ivan Seaton:

Residence: 1957   Chatham-Kent, Kent, Ontario, Canada[155]
                 HH: Harold Seaton (labourer); Audrey

Residence: 1963   Chatham-Kent, Kent, Ontario, Canada[155]
                 HH: Harold Campbell (Garage operator); Audrey (stenographer)

Residence: 1974   Chatham-Kent, Kent, Ontario, Canada[155]
                 HH: Harold Campbell (garage operator); Mrs Audrey (secretary)

[153] Ancestry.com, Canada, Selected School Yearbooks, 1908-2010 (Provo, UT, USA, Ancestry.com Operations, Inc., 2015), Ancestry.com, "Canada, Selected School Yearbooks, 1908-2010"; School: London Normal School; Year: 1951.
[Source citation includes one media item]

[154] Ancestry.com, Canada, Find A Grave Index, 1600s-Current (Provo, UT, USA, Ancestry.com Operations, Inc., 2012), Ancestry.com.

[155] Ancestry.com, Canada, Voters Lists, 1935-1980 (Provo, UT, USA, Ancestry.com Operations, Inc., 2012), Ancestry.com, Library and Archives Canada; Ottawa, Ontario, Canada; Voters Lists, Federal Elections, 1935-1980.
[Source citation includes one media item]

Figure 51: Brussells Cemetery

William Campbell

1313. **William Alfred[5] Campbell** was born on Friday, April 24, 1931, in West Lorne, Elgin, Ontario, Canada.[156, 157] He was the son of Gordon Campbell Pusey and Charlotte Ann Mills (131).

William Alfred retired in Toronto, Ontario, Canada, in 1996. Retired from Toronto Transit Commission. He died at Mt. Sinai Hospital, Toronto in Toronto, Ontario, Canada, on June 17, 2004, at the age of 73.[156, 157] William Alfred was buried at Chatham (55 Maple Leaf Dr,   Chatham, Chatham-Kent Municipality, Ontario, Canada) in Chatham-Kent, Kent, Ontario, Canada, on July 10, 2004.[156]

Marriages with Barbara J Byron and Doreen Codner (Page 98) are known.

Figure 52: Maple Leaf Cemetery

[156] Ancestry.com, Canada Obituary Collection (Provo, UT, USA, Ancestry.com Operations Inc, 2006), Ancestry.com, Publication Place: Canada; URL: http://www.inmemoriam.ca/view-announcement-129405-william-alfred-campbell.html.

[157] Ancestry.com, Web: Obituary Daily Times Index, 1995-2012 (Provo, UT, USA, Ancestry.com Operations, Inc., 2012), Ancestry.com.

Family of William Campbell and Barbara Byron

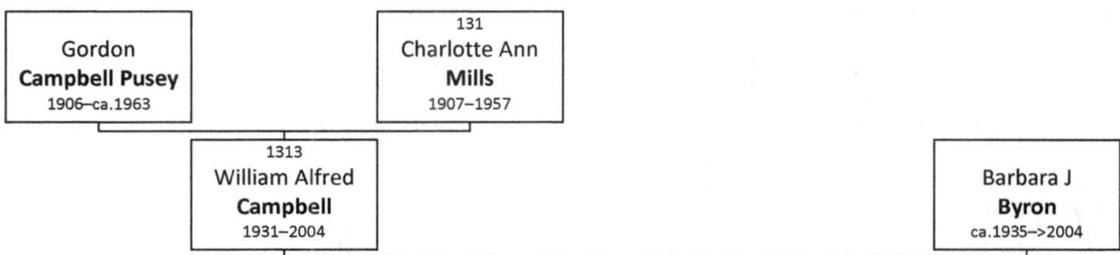

Here are the details about **William Alfred Campbell's** first marriage with Barbara J Byron. You can read more about William Alfred on page 96.

Barbara J Byron was born at (Likely) in Ontario, Canada, about 1935. Barbara J died after 2004.

More facts and events for Barbara J Byron:

Residence: June 17, 2004   Durham, Ontario, Canada
Residence cited in William Alfred Campbell obituary.

Family of William Campbell and Doreen Codner

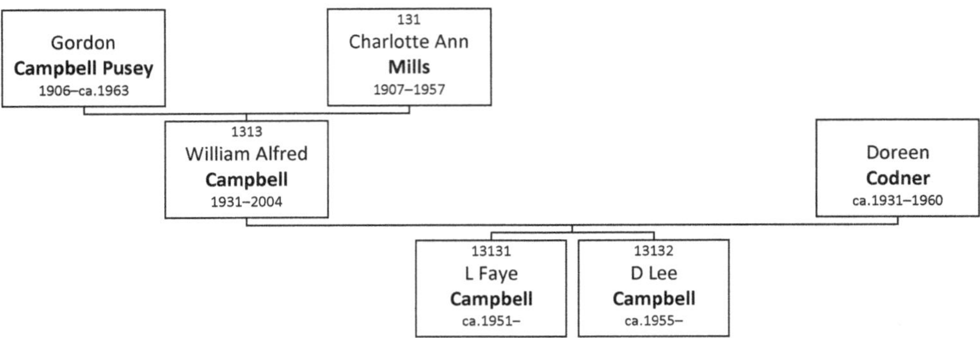

Here are the details about **William Alfred Campbell's** second marriage with Doreen Codner. You can read more about William Alfred on page 96.

They had two children: L (ca.1951–) and D (ca.1955–). Doreen Codner was born at (Likely) in Elgin, Ontario, Canada, about 1931.

Doreen reached 29 years of age and died in 1960.

L Campbell

13131. **L Faye[6] Campbell** was born about 1951.[158] She is the daughter of William Alfred Campbell (1313) and Doreen Codner.

More facts and events for L Faye Campbell:

Residence: June 17, 2004   Nova Scotia, Canada
Residence cited in William Alfred Campbell obituary.

Marriages with (unknown given name) Johnson and Thomas Begin (Page 101) are known.

---

158   Ancestry.com, Canada, Find A Grave Index, 1600s-Current (Provo, UT, USA, Ancestry.com Operations, Inc., 2012), Ancestry.com.

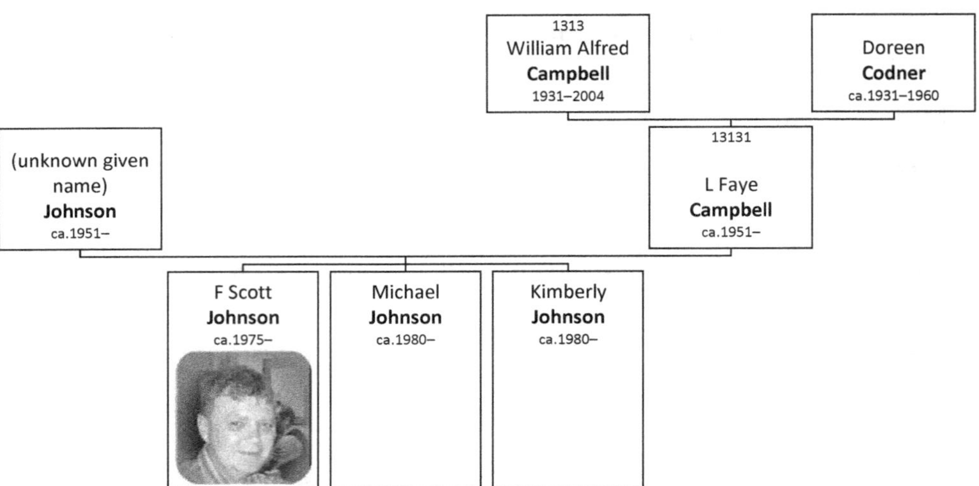

Here are the details about **L Faye Campbell's** first marriage with (unknown given name) Johnson. You can read more about L Faye on page 99.

They have three children: F (ca.1975–), Michael (ca.1980–) and Kimberly (ca.1980–). (unknown given name) Johnson was born at (Likely) in Ontario, Canada, about 1951.

Family of L Campbell and Thomas Begin

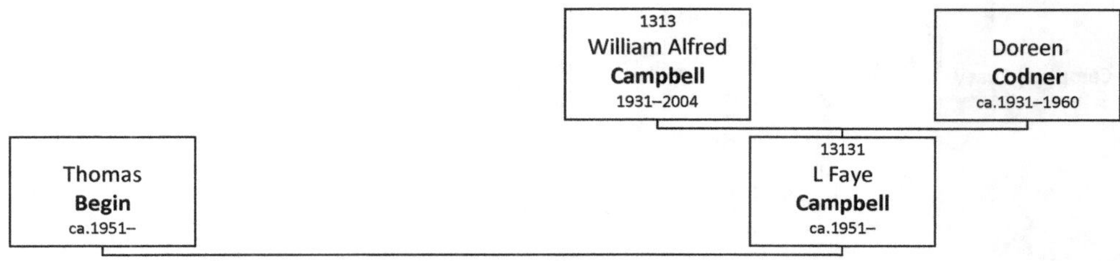

Here are the details about **L Faye Campbell's** second marriage with Thomas Begin. You can read more about L Faye on page 99.

Thomas Begin was born at (Likely) in Ontario, Canada, about 1951.

More facts and events for Thomas Begin:

Residence: June 17, 2004   Nova Scotia, Canada
Residence cited in William Alfred Campbell obituary.

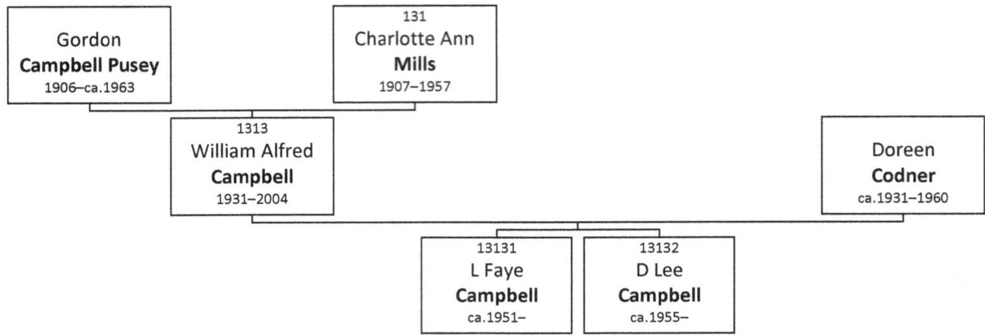

13132. D Lee[6] **Campbell** was born about 1955 at (Likely) in Elgin, Ontario, Canada. He is the son of William Alfred Campbell (1313) and Doreen Codner.

More facts and events for D Lee Campbell:

Residence: June 17, 2004   Guelph, Wellington, Ontario, Canada
Residence cited in William Alfred Campbell obituary.

Family of Arthur Campbell and Rose ()

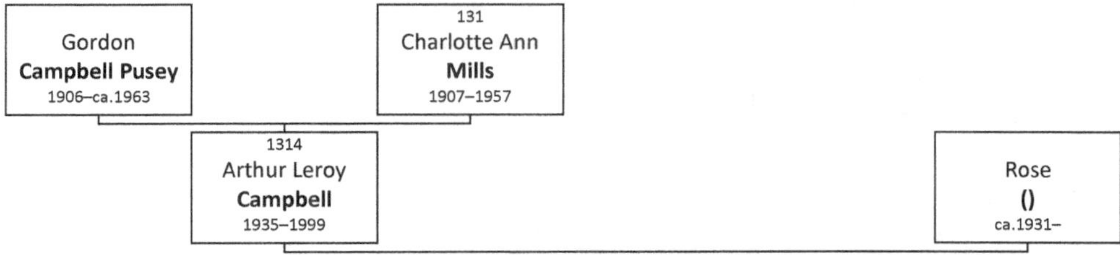

1314. **Arthur Leroy**[5] **Campbell** was born on Sunday, September 15, 1935.[159] He was the son of Gordon Campbell Pusey and Charlotte Ann Mills (131).

Arthur Leroy died at Chatham in Chatham-Kent, Kent, Ontario, Canada, on June 23, 1999, at the age of 63.[159] He was buried at Chatham (Maple Leaf Cemetery, Chatham, Chatham-Kent Municipality, Ontario, Canada) in Chatham-Kent, Kent, Ontario, Canada.[159]

More facts and events for Arthur Leroy Campbell:

Residence: 1968   Chatham-Kent, Kent, Ontario, Canada[160]
              HH: Arthur Campbell (maintenance); Rose

Rose () was born at (Likely) (HH: Arthur Campbell (maintenance); Rose) in Ontario, Canada, about 1931.

More facts and events for Rose ():

Residence: 1968   Chatham-Kent, Kent, Ontario, Canada[160]

Figure 53: Arthur Leroy Campbell

Figure 54: Chatham Cemetery

---

[159]   Ancestry.com, Canada, Find A Grave Index, 1600s-Current (Provo, UT, USA, Ancestry.com Operations, Inc., 2012), Ancestry.com.

[160]   Ancestry.com, Canada, Voters Lists, 1935-1980 (Provo, UT, USA, Ancestry.com Operations, Inc., 2012), Ancestry.com, Library and Archives Canada; Ottawa, Ontario, Canada; Voters Lists, Federal Elections, 1935-1980.
[Source citation includes one media item]

Family of Sarah Mills and Francis Crawford

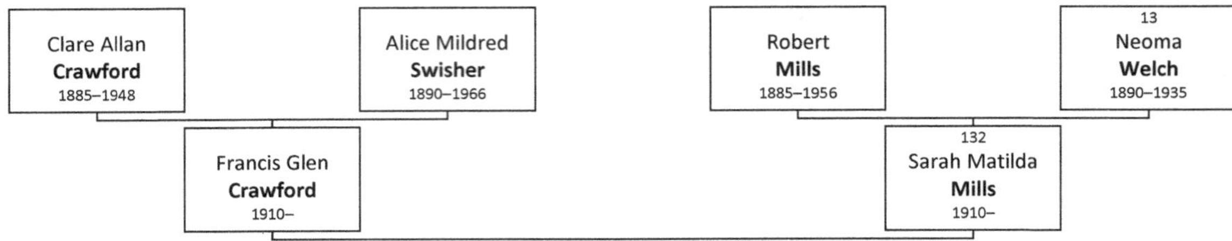

132. **Sarah Matilda[4] Mills** was born on Monday, April 11, 1910, in West Lorne, Elgin, Ontario, Canada.[161–164] She is the daughter of Robert Mills and Neoma Welch (13).

More facts and events for Sarah Matilda Mills:

Residence: 1911	West Lorne, Elgin, Ontario, Canada[162] Single; Dau / Cohab: Robert Mills 25, Reoma Mills 21, Charlotte Ann Mills 3, Sarah Matilda Mills 1.	
Residence: June 1, 1921	West Lorne, Elgin, Ontario, Canada[163] Baptist; Single; : Dau/ Cohab: Robert Mills 36, Neoma Mills 28, Lotty Mills 13, Motile Mills 11, Robert Mills 10, Mirtle Mills 7, Mary Mills 8/12.	
Residence: 1935	Rodney, Elgin, Ontario, Canada[165] HH: Clare Crawford (clerk); Mrs Clare ()married woman); Glen (labourer), Mrs Glen (married woman)	
Residence: 1945	Rodney, Elgin, Ontario, Canada[165] HH: Allan Crawford (Clerk); Mrs Allan; Glen (factory worker); Mrs Glen	
Residence: 1958	Rodney, Elgin, Ontario, Canada[165] HH: Glen Crawford (factory empl); Mrs Glen	
Residence: 1962	Rodney, Elgin, Ontario, Canada[165] HH: Glen Crawford (factory empl); Mrs Glen	
Residence: 1972	Rodney, Elgin, Ontario, Canada[165] HH: Glen Crawford (labourer); Mrs Glen	

Francis Glen Crawford was born in Kent, Ontario, Canada, on Tuesday, March 15, 1910.[164, 166–168] He is the son of Clare Allan Crawford and Alice Mildred Swisher.

161 Ancestry.com, Ontario, Canada Births, 1869-1913 (Provo, UT, USA, Ancestry.com Operations Inc, 2010), Ancestry.com, Archives of Ontario; Toronto, Ontario, Canada; Delayed Registrations and Stillbirths, "50" Series, 1869-1911, 1913; Series: MS930; Reel: 61; Record Group: RG 80-2.
[Source citation includes one media item]

162 Ancestry.com, 1911 Census of Canada (Provo, UT, USA, Ancestry.com Operations Inc, 2006), Ancestry.com, Year: 1911; Census Place: 41 - West Lorne, Elgin West, Ontario; Page: 8; Family No: 100.
[Source citation includes one media item]

163 Ancestry.com, 1921 Census of Canada (Provo, UT, USA, Ancestry.com Operations Inc, 2013), Ancestry.com, Reference Number: RG 31; Folder Number: 56; Census Place: 56, Elgin West, Ontario; Page Number: 2.
[Source citation includes one media item]

164 Ancestry.com and Genealogical Research Library (Brampton, Ontario, Canada), Ontario, Canada, Marriages, 1801-1928 (Provo, UT, USA, Ancestry.com Operations, Inc., 2010), Ancestry.com, Archives of Ontario; Toronto, Ontario, Canada; Series: MS 932; Reel: 891.
[Source citation includes one media item]

165 Ancestry.com, Canada, Voters Lists, 1935-1980 (Provo, UT, USA, Ancestry.com Operations, Inc., 2012), Ancestry.com, Library and Archives Canada; Ottawa, Ontario, Canada; Voters Lists, Federal Elections, 1935-1980.
[Source citation includes one media item]

More facts and events for Francis Glen Crawford:

Residence:	1911	Kent, Ontario, Canada[168]
		Presbyterian; Single; Son / HH: Elair Crawford 34, Alis Mildred Crawford 11, Francis Glen Crawford 1, Lele S Duncan Crawford 2/12.
Residence:	June 1, 1921	Rodney, Elgin, Ontario, Canada[167]
		Presbyterian; Single; Son; Public School Student / HH: Clare Crawford 35, Alice Crawford 30, Glen Crawford 11, Allen Crawford 10.
Residence:	1935	Rodney, Elgin, Ontario, Canada[165]
		HH: Clare Crawford (clerk); Mrs Clare ()married woman); Glen (labourer), Mrs Glen (married woman)
Residence:	1945	Rodney, Elgin, Ontario, Canada[165]
		HH: Allan Crawford (Clerk); Mrs Allan; Glen (factory worker); Mrs Glen
Residence:	1958	Rodney, Elgin, Ontario, Canada[165]
		HH: Glen Crawford (factory empl); Mrs Glen
Residence:	1962	Rodney, Elgin, Ontario, Canada[165]
		HH: Glen Crawford (factory empl); Mrs Glen
Residence:	1963	Rodney, Elgin, Ontario, Canada[165]
		HH: Glen Crawford (factory empl); Mrs Glen
Residence:	1972	Rodney, Elgin, Ontario, Canada[165]
		HH: Glen Crawford (labourer); Mrs Glen

[166]   Ancestry.com, Ontario, Canada Births, 1869-1913 (Provo, UT, USA, Ancestry.com Operations Inc, 2010), Ancestry.com, Archives of Ontario; Toronto, Ontario, Canada; Registrations of Births and Stillbirths, 1869-1913; Series: MS929; Reel: 210; Record Group: RG 80-2.
[Source citation includes one media item]

[167]   Ancestry.com, 1921 Census of Canada (Provo, UT, USA, Ancestry.com Operations Inc, 2013), Ancestry.com, Reference Number: RG 31; Folder Number: 56; Census Place: 56, Elgin West, Ontario; Page Number: 13.
[Source citation includes one media item]

[168]   Ancestry.com, 1911 Census of Canada (Provo, UT, USA, Ancestry.com Operations Inc, 2006), Ancestry.com, Year: 1911; Census Place: 31 - Orford Township, Duart Village, Kent East, Ontario; Page: 6; Family No: 54.
[Source citation includes one media item]

Robert Mills

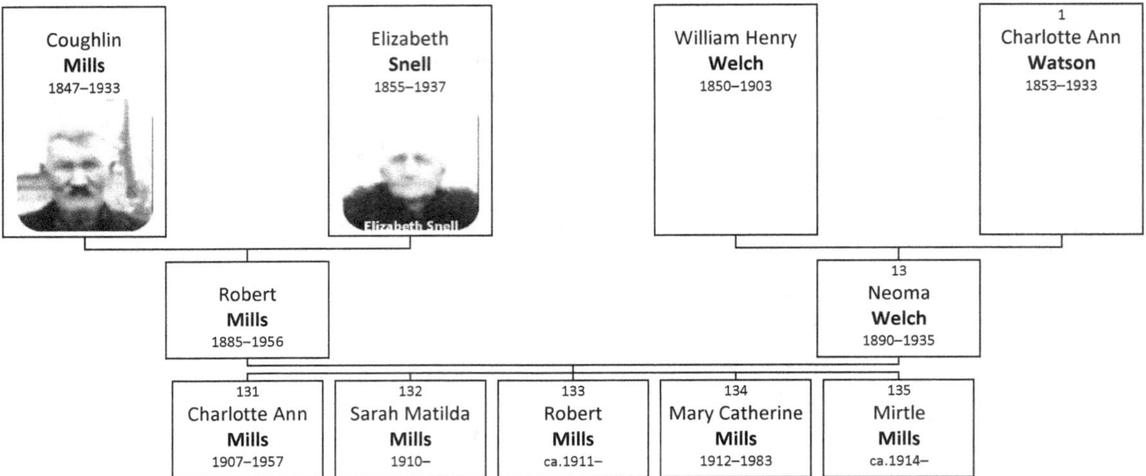

133.   **Robert**[4] **Mills** was born about 1911 in Ontario, Canada.[169] He is the son of Robert Mills and Neoma Welch (13).

More facts and events for Robert Mills:

Residence: June 1, 1921   West Lorne, Elgin, Ontario, Canada[169]
Baptist;   Single;   Son/ Cohab: Robert Mills 36,   Neoma Mills 28,   Lotty Mills 13,   Motile Mills 11,   Robert Mills 10,   Mirtle Mills 7,   Mary Mills 8/12.

---

169   Ancestry.com, 1921 Census of Canada (Provo, UT, USA, Ancestry.com Operations Inc, 2013), Ancestry.com, Reference Number: RG 31; Folder Number: 56; Census Place: 56, Elgin West, Ontario; Page Number: 2.
[Source citation includes one media item]

Family of Mary Mills and William Paterson

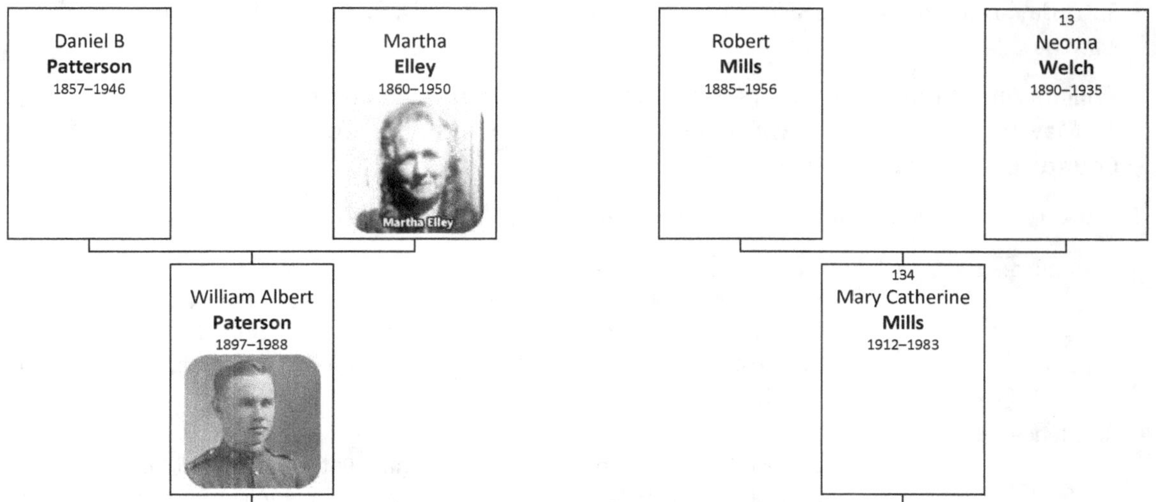

134. **Mary Catherine[4] Mills** was born on Friday, February 23, 1912, in St Thomas, Elgin, Ontario, Canada.[170–174] She was the daughter of Robert Mills and Neoma Welch (13).

Mary Catherine died in London, Middlesex, Ontario, Canada, on February 25, 1983, at the age of 71.[173, 174] She was buried at McLean Cemetery,   West Elgin, Elgin County, Ontario, Canad in Elgin, Ontario, Canada.[173, 174]

More facts and events for Mary Catherine Mills:

Residence: June 1, 1921   West Lorne, Elgin, Ontario, Canada[172]
Baptist;   Single;   Dau / HH: Robert Mills 36,   Neoma Mills 28,   Lotty Mills 13, Motile Mills 11,   Robert Mills 10,   Mirtle Mills 7,   Mary Mills 8/12.

[170] Ancestry.com and Genealogical Research Library (Brampton, Ontario, Canada), Ontario, Canada, Marriages, 1801-1928 (Provo, UT, USA, Ancestry.com Operations, Inc., 2010), Ancestry.com, Archives of Ontario; Toronto, Ontario, Canada; Registration of Marriages 1936; Reel: 14-333.
[Source citation includes one media item]

[171] Ancestry.com, Ontario, Canada Births, 1869-1913 (Provo, UT, USA, Ancestry.com Operations Inc, 2010), Ancestry.com, Archives of Ontario; Toronto, Ontario, Canada; Registrations of Births and Stillbirths, 1869-1913; Series: MS929; Reel: 226; Record Group: RG 80-2.
[Source citation includes one media item]

[172] Ancestry.com, 1921 Census of Canada (Provo, UT, USA, Ancestry.com Operations Inc, 2013), Ancestry.com, Reference Number: RG 31; Folder Number: 56; Census Place: 56, Elgin West, Ontario; Page Number: 2.
[Source citation includes one media item]

[173] Ancestry.com, Web: Canada, GenWeb Cemetery Index (Provo, UT, USA, Ancestry.com Operations, Inc., 2013), Ancestry.com.

[174] Ancestry.com, Canada, Find A Grave Index, 1600s-Current (Provo, UT, USA, Ancestry.com Operations, Inc., 2012), Ancestry.com.

William Albert Paterson was born at Aldborough in Elgin, Ontario, Canada, on Saturday, December 18, 1897.[170, 173–181] He was the son of Daniel B Patterson and Martha Elley.

William Albert reached 90 years of age and died in Rodney, Elgin, Ontario, Canada, on May 16, 1988.[173, 174] He was buried at McLean Cemetery,   West Elgin, Elgin County, Ontario, Canada in Elgin, Ontario, Canada.[173, 174]

William Albert Paterson

More facts and events for William Albert Paterson:

Residence: 1901   Elgin, Ontario, Canada[177]
Single; Son / HH: Daniel Paterson 43,   Martha Patterson 40,   Mary T Patterson 15,   Dan A Patterson 14,   Peter J Patterson 12,   Dane J Patterson 10,   James E Patterson 8,   Jennie B Patterson 6,   William A Patterson 3,   Arch G Patterson 11/12.

Residence: 1911   Elgin, Ontario, Canada[176]
Baptist; Single;   Son; farmer / HH: Donald Patterson 53,   Martha Patterson 50,   Peter J Patterson 22,   James A Patterson 18,   Jennie B Patterson 16,   William A Patterson 13,   Archibald G Patterson 12,   Mable Edna Patterson 10,   Lily Irene Patterson 6.

Residence: June 3, 1916   Chatham-Kent, Kent, Ontario, Canada[180]
5' 7", blue eyes, brown hair

Residence: June 1, 1921   Elgin, Ontario, Canada[179]
Baptist;   Single;   Son; farmer / HH: Daniel Patterson 63,   Martha Patterson 60,   William A Patterson 23,   Mable Patterson 19,   Lillie Patterson 16.

175   Ancestry.com and Genealogical Research Library (Brampton, Ontario, Canada), Ontario, Canada, Marriages, 1801-1928 (Provo, UT, USA, Ancestry.com Operations, Inc., 2010), Ancestry.com, Archives of Ontario; Toronto, Ontario, Canada; Registrations of Marriages, 1869-1928; Reel: 677.
[Source citation includes one media item]

176   Ancestry.com, 1911 Census of Canada (Provo, UT, USA, Ancestry.com Operations Inc, 2006), Ancestry.com, Year: 1911; Census Place: 5 - Aldborough, Elgin West, Ontario; Page: 1; Family No: 4.
[Source citation includes one media item]

177   Ancestry.com, 1901 Census of Canada (Provo, UT, USA, Ancestry.com Operations Inc, 2006), Ancestry.com, Year: 1901; Census Place: Aldborough, Elgin (West/Ouest), Ontario; Page: 1; Family No: 7.
[Source citation includes one media item]

178   Ancestry.com, Ontario, Canada Births, 1869-1913 (Provo, UT, USA, Ancestry.com Operations Inc, 2010), Ancestry.com, Archives of Ontario; Toronto, Ontario, Canada; Registrations of Births and Stillbirths, 1869-1913; Series: MS929; Reel: 142; Record Group: RG 80-2.
[Source citation includes one media item]

179   Ancestry.com, 1921 Census of Canada (Provo, UT, USA, Ancestry.com Operations Inc, 2013), Ancestry.com, Reference Number: RG 31; Folder Number: 55; Census Place: 55, Elgin West, Ontario; Page Number: 8.
[Source citation includes one media item]

180   Ancestry.com, Canada, WWI CEF Personnel Files, 1914-1918 (Lehi, UT, USA, Ancestry.com Operations, Inc., 2016), Ancestry.com, Library and Archives Canada; Ottawa, Ontario, Canada; CEF Personnel Files; Reference: RG 150; Volume: Box 7652 - 5.
[Source citation includes one media item]

181   Ancestry.com, Canada, Soldiers of the First World War, 1914-1918 (Provo, UT, USA, Ancestry.com Operations, Inc., 2006), Ancestry.com.
[Source citation includes one media item]

Figure 55: McLean Cemetery

Mirtle Mills

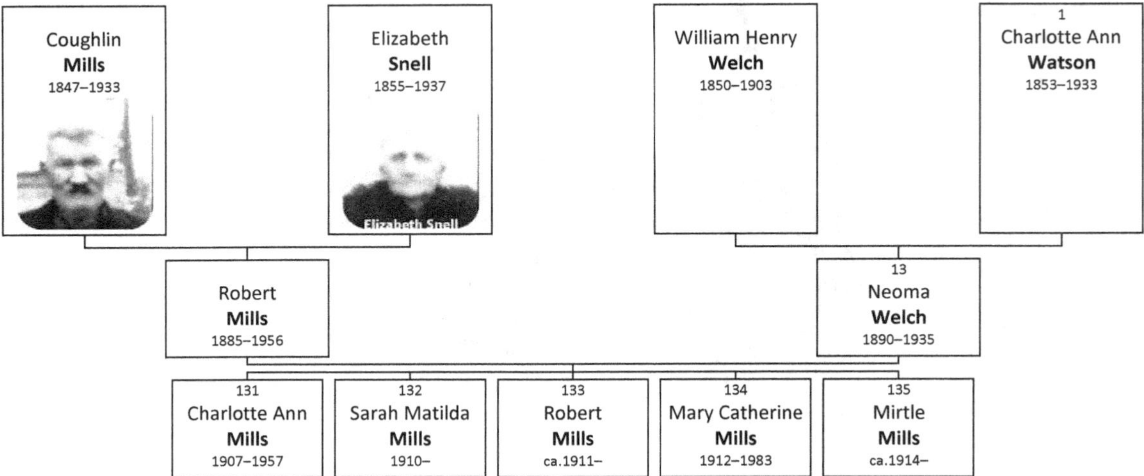

135. **Mirtle[4] Mills** was born about 1914 at (Likely) in West Lorne, Elgin, Ontario, Canada.[182] She is the daughter of Robert Mills and Neoma Welch (13).

More facts and events for Mirtle Mills:

Residence: June 1, 1921   West Lorne, Elgin, Ontario, Canada[182]
Baptist;   Single;   Dau / HH: Robert Mills 36,   Neoma Mills 28,   Lotty Mills 13,   Motile Mills 11,   Robert Mills 10,   Mirtle Mills 7,   Mary Mills 8/12.

---

182   Ancestry.com, 1921 Census of Canada (Provo, UT, USA, Ancestry.com Operations Inc, 2013), Ancestry.com, Reference Number: RG 31; Folder Number: 56; Census Place: 56, Elgin West, Ontario; Page Number: 2.
[Source citation includes one media item]

Bibliography

Ancestry.com and Genealogical Research Library (Brampton, Ontario, Canada). *Ontario, Canada, Marriages, 1801-1928*. Provo, UT, USA: Ancestry.com Operations, Inc., 2010.

Ancestry.com and The Church of Jesus Christ of Latter-day Saints. *1861 Census of Canada*. Provo, UT, USA: Ancestry.com Operations Inc, 2009.

Ancestry.com and The Church of Jesus Christ of Latter-day Saints. *1871 Census of Canada*. Provo, UT, USA: Ancestry.com Operations Inc, 2009.

Ancestry.com. *1851 Census of Canada East, Canada West, New Brunswick, and Nova Scotia*. Provo, UT, USA: Ancestry.com Operations Inc, 2006.

Ancestry.com. *1891 Census of Canada*. Provo, UT, USA: Ancestry.com Operations Inc, 2008.

Ancestry.com. *1901 Census of Canada*. Provo, UT, USA: Ancestry.com Operations Inc, 2006.

Ancestry.com. *1911 Census of Canada*. Provo, UT, USA: Ancestry.com Operations Inc, 2006.

Ancestry.com. *1921 Census of Canada*. Provo, UT, USA: Ancestry.com Operations Inc, 2013.

Ancestry.com. *1940 United States Federal Census*. Provo, UT, USA: Ancestry.com Operations, Inc., 2012.

Ancestry.com. *Beta: Newspapers.com Obituary Index, 1940-1955*. Lehi, UT, USA: Ancestry.com Operations Inc, 2019.

Ancestry.com. *Border Crossings: From Canada to U.S., 1895-1956*. Provo, UT, USA: Ancestry.com Operations, Inc., 2010.

Ancestry.com. *Canada Obituary Collection*. Provo, UT, USA: Ancestry.com Operations Inc, 2006.

Ancestry.com. *Canada, Find A Grave Index, 1600s-Current*. Provo, UT, USA: Ancestry.com Operations, Inc., 2012.

Ancestry.com. *Canada, Selected School Yearbooks, 1908-2010*. Provo, UT, USA: Ancestry.com Operations, Inc., 2015.

Ancestry.com. *Canada, Soldiers of the First World War, 1914-1918*. Provo, UT, USA: Ancestry.com Operations, Inc., 2006.

Ancestry.com. *Canada, Voters Lists, 1935-1980*. Provo, UT, USA: Ancestry.com Operations, Inc., 2012.

Ancestry.com. *Canada, WWI CEF Personnel Files, 1914-1918*. Lehi, UT, USA: Ancestry.com Operations, Inc., 2016.

Ancestry.com. *Canada, WWII Service Files of War Dead, 1939-1947*. Provo, UT, USA: Ancestry Operations, Inc., 2015.

Ancestry.com. *Canadian Passenger Lists, 1865-1935*. Provo, UT, USA: Ancestry.com Operations Inc, 2010.

Ancestry.com. *Canadian Phone and Address Directories, 1995-2002*. Provo, UT, USA: Ancestry.com Operations Inc, 2005.

Ancestry.com. *Detroit Border Crossings and Passenger and Crew Lists, 1905-1957*. Provo, UT, USA: Ancestry.com Operations Inc, 2006.

Ancestry.com. *England & Wales, Death Index, 1916-2007*. Provo, UT, USA: Ancestry.com Operations Inc, 2007.

Ancestry.com. *International, Find A Grave Index for Select Locations, 1300s-Current*. Provo, UT, USA: Ancestry.com Operations, Inc., 2012.

Ancestry.com. *Michigan, Marriage Records, 1867-1952*. Provo, UT, USA: Ancestry.com Operations, Inc., 2015.

Ancestry.com. *New York State, Birth Index, 1881-1942*. Lehi, UT, USA: Ancestry.com Operations, Inc., 2018.

Ancestry.com. *Ohio Marriage Index, 1970, 1972-2007*. Provo, UT: Ancestry.com Operations, Inc, 2010.

Ancestry.com. *Ontario, Canada Births, 1869-1913*. Provo, UT, USA: Ancestry.com Operations Inc, 2010.

Ancestry.com. *Ontario, Canada, Deaths, 1869-1938 and Deaths Overseas, 1939-1947*. Provo, UT, USA: Ancestry.com Operations Inc, 2010.

Ancestry.com. *U.S. Cemetery and Funeral Home Collection*. Provo, UT, USA: Ancestry.com Operations Inc, 2011.

Ancestry.com. *U.S. City Directories, 1821-1989*. Provo, UT, USA: Ancestry.com Operations, Inc., 2011.

Ancestry.com. *U.S. Phone and Address Directories, 1993-2002*. Provo, UT, USA: Ancestry.com Operations Inc, 2005.

Ancestry.com. *U.S. Public Records Index, Volume 1*. Provo, UT, USA: Ancestry.com Operations, Inc., 2010.

Ancestry.com. *U.S. Public Records Index, Volume 2*. Provo, UT, USA: Ancestry.com Operations, Inc., 2010.

Ancestry.com. *U.S. School Yearbooks*. Provo, UT, USA: Ancestry.com Operations, Inc., 2010.

Ancestry.com. *U.S. WWII Draft Cards Young Men, 1940-1947*. Provo, UT, USA: Ancestry.com Operations, Inc., 2011.

Ancestry.com. *U.S., Find A Grave Index, 1700s-Current*. Provo, UT, USA: Ancestry.com Operations, Inc., 2012.

Ancestry.com. *U.S., Railroad Retirement Pension Index, 1934-1987*. Lehi, UT, USA: Ancestry.com Operations, Inc., 2017.

Ancestry.com. *U.S., Social Security Applications and Claims Index, 1936-2007*. Provo, UT, USA: Ancestry.com Operations, Inc., 2015.

Ancestry.com. *U.S., Social Security Death Index, 1935-Current*. Provo, UT, USA: Ancestry.com Operations Inc, 2011.

Ancestry.com. *UK and Ireland, Find A Grave Index, 1300s-Current*. Provo, UT, USA: Ancestry.com Operations, Inc., 2012.

Ancestry.com. *Web: Canada, GenWeb Cemetery Index*. Provo, UT, USA: Ancestry.com Operations, Inc., 2013.

Ancestry.com. *Web: Canada, Virtual War Memorial Index, 1900-2014*. Lehi, UT, USA: Ancestry.com Operations, Inc., 2016.

Ancestry.com. *Web: CanadianHeadstones.com Index*. Provo, UT, USA: Ancestry.com Operations, Inc., 2012.

Ancestry.com. *Web: Obituary Daily Times Index, 1995-2012*. Provo, UT, USA: Ancestry.com Operations, Inc., 2012.

Index of Places

USA, New York, Orleans, Medina

(43.2201° N, 78.387° W)

USA, North Carolina, Alexander, Taylorsville

(35.9218° N, 81.1765° W)

USA, North Carolina, Mecklenburg, Charlotte

(35.2271° N, 80.8432° W)

USA, Ohio, Delaware, Lewis Center

USA, South Carolina

USA, South Carolina, Greenville

(34.8931° N, 82.3708° W)

USA, South Carolina, Greenville, Fountain Inn

(34.6889° N, 82.1958° W)

USA, South Carolina, Greenville, Greer

(34.9406° N, 82.2315° W)

USA, South Carolina, Greenville, Mauldin

(34.7787° N, 82.3101° W)

USA, South Carolina, Greenville, Simpsonville

(34.7371° N, 82.2543° W)

USA, South Carolina, Lexington

USA, South Carolina, Lexington, Columbia

(33.9986° N, 81.0452° W)

USA, South Carolina, Richland, Columbia

(34.0007° N, 81.0348° W)

Index of Individuals

www.ingramcontent.com/pod-product-compliance
Lightning Source LLC
Chambersburg PA
CBHW081725250726
48657CB00010B/3128